HU$TLE

A GUIDE TO THE ETHICAL ART OF SELLING & SURVIVAL

HU$TLE

DENNIS PLINTZ

DP Ventures Inc. | Calgary

Editing by Zoey Duncan (ZoeyWrites.com)
Book design by Zoey Duncan
Cover design by Avanska
Published by DP Ventures Inc.

Library and Archives Canada Cataloguing in Publication

Plintz, Dennis, author
      Hustle : a guide to the ethical art of selling & survival
/ Dennis Plintz -- First edition.

ISBN 978-0-9950746-0-6 (hardback)

      1. Plintz, Dennis. 2. Sales personnel--Biography.
3. Businesspeople--Biography. 4. Selling--Psychological
aspects. 5. Success in business. I. Title.

HF5439.32.P55A3 2016   658.85   C2016-901755-9

Printed in Canada.
First Edition

For my mom; my hero.

Thank you for teaching me forgiveness, giving, how to live in contentment and how to always be thankful despite difficult circumstances.

And thank you especially for buying me Optimus Prime when I was 11 despite not being remotely able to afford it.

You have always kept me in pursuit of all this great life has to offer.

CONTENTS

Introduction

"Just remember, the sweet is never as sweet without the sour, and I know the sour."

—Brian Shelby, in Vanilla Sky

THERE'S NO SUCH THING AS A LUCKY LIFE

The greatest gift I've been given is the upbringing I had. I have to say that now because if you read the next chapter about what my childhood was like, you might not believe me.

From the outside, mine was an upbringing plenty of people would call less fortunate. I would say it was full of fortune. In fact, it perfectly positioned me to get on the rocket ship I'm currently riding.

Growing up without much of anything meant every little bit we did have mattered tremendously. Bread that wasn't mouldy and milk that wasn't sour were wins. The opportunity—sometimes—to have butter on that bread and chocolate syrup for the milk was a celebration in our home.

Today, to be debt-free with money in the bank and a car

feels like a dream. It's a lifetime of difference. And my diversity of experience in one lifetime means now I can sit with almost any individual in a sales relationship and get them.

Trial and error taught me there is a formula to my success and it has everything to do with consistent hard work and the relentless pursuit of better. A few years into my sales career, though, I worried my success to that point was all luck.

Having "good luck" was terrifying for me. It implied success happened by chance, rather than by anything I did. Meaning I might never be able to replicate it.

My unhealthy fear of luck lurked in the back of my mind until about five years into my real estate career. Around that time I realized I was still pretty successful, and it was, in fact, because of what I was doing. I was hustling.

I've come to understand the people who we perceive as "lucky" in life are people who focus on opportunity and seek more of it despite the struggle along the way. Life itself is a challenge filled with obstacles and opportunities, light and darkness, pleasure and pain.

I struggled for a while to find the right fit for my level of hustle. I was making people's dentures before I was introduced professionally to sales, selling pots and pans to people in their homes. My first year as a pots and pans salesman, I doubled my income compared to when I was in the dental industry. Yeah, it was a massive lift in my income, but the more exciting aspect of the shift for me was the feeling I experienced when I started relying fully on commission sales. I call it "fearful independence." It was terrifying and completely rewarding at the same time. I was free from the 9-to-5 grind, but forever a victim of uncertainty. I'd be relying on my hustle to get me through. The uncertainty is completely worth it. It's been a hell of a ride and I wouldn't trade it for anything.

I started my real estate business in 2003 following five years of selling pots and pans. I made the Million Dollar Club[*] in 2004 and I've grown my business every year since. I was named one of the Top 21 real estate agents in the country in 2009 and smashed my sales targets that year. In the years that followed, I was amongst the top 2% of real estate agents in our marketplace for residential real estate.

My team continues working to grow the business. We do a lot, from first-time single homebuyers to some of the most expensive real estate in the country. We sell individual condos and complete land assemblies.

I got where I am because of where I have been. I can stand in line at the food bank and strike up a conversation that's as meaningful as the one I have while boarding first class with my

---

* The Calgary Real Estate Board has since eliminated the "Million Dollar Club" Award. This was an award that many agents (myself included) strived towards achieving. Being a member of this club meant you were in the top 2-3% of the market based on sales.

family. That's thanks to how I was brought up, especially my quest for security as a young boy. That's when I started learning to hustle.

When I was a kid, there were a lot of scary days, like those spent waiting in the emergency room with Mom thanks to a bad boyfriend. But then there was the amazing Christmas dinner we had when I was nine years old. We went to McDonald's first, because it was the only restaurant my mom thought would be open on Dec. 25. It wasn't, so she brought us instead to a steakhouse—the best restaurant around—and spent money she didn't really have. It was the first Christmas I remember celebrating with both my brother and my mom. It didn't matter where we were, it just mattered we were together and safe at that point in our lives.

Mom always seemed to find ways to do special things for us, things that might have seemed insignificant to other people. But she had a knack for making the small wins feel massive. Every little bit really mattered. Still today, the smallest victories feel like home runs to me.

I've experienced both the sweet and the sour. The dark places in life have given me a better appreciation for the light. Each taste of something better drives me to embrace and share all that is amazing.

Having been through some dark days, I know the sun will

rise tomorrow. But how happy I am to see that sun depends on my level of hustle.

By "hustle," I mean my willingness to get up every day and seek out every opportunity to improve on yesterday.

Hustle is the relentless pursuit of better despite a reality of difficulty plus the gratitude to appreciate every bit of it. And hustling is the relentless pursuit of the best version of myself, a version I know is possible despite how the world may treat me.

I vividly remember the morning social services came to our house to take away my brother and I from Mom. My brother Daren was nine; I was just four.

Kicking and screaming, I used every ounce of strength to cling to Mom. We were desperate to explain to the social services people what seemed so obvious to us kids: you shouldn't take us away from our mom.

They overpowered us. Ripped us from the comfort of her arms. We didn't know they were taking us to a new life of unfamiliar faces. It was the start of a new path where most of life's lessons would be learned the hard way.

I didn't feel lucky that day.

I was very young, but it didn't take long for me to realize I had to do something to make my situation better. I needed to wear as big a smile as possible and tread lightly. I like to call it "living with optimism, through a filter of skepticism."

I learned when to shut up and when to speak up.

When to fight and when to take a beating.

When to put on a smile and when to push back.

I figured out the rules, played by them and broke them if necessary.

I learned the art of survival.

It turns out I learned the art of selling.

Finding a career in sales that works for me wasn't easy, but it was without a doubt the greatest move I've ever made to make money and build meaningful relationships.

I guess you can say this square peg has found his corresponding square hole.

The stories that follow are the ones that made me and continue to make me. I will tap into them for the rest of my existence and I've collected them here because I'm not the only one who has had a bumpy journey.

All of life is selling, and it's much easier to live—and sell—when you're comfortable with your story. Owning my story has not only allowed me to appreciate how I got to where I am, but has freed me to dig deeper, live bigger and feel freer.

I read it somewhere that your future will be determined by the quality of your consciousness. I believe the quality of my consciousness depends on how I tell my own story to myself.

Everyone experiences pain and loss. What we tell ourselves

about the pain and loss determines the effect it has on us.

It's all energy. Find a way to be propelled by it.

You can use your story to sell your way to a better future.

If you've already got a view from the top, then hopefully this book will help you stay there while providing some context for what the bottom looks like. It might remind you how exciting, difficult and worthwhile the journey was, and why we need to help others experience their own journey.

If you're at the bottom? Let these stories be your proof: you can turn whatever you've got into something more, and then do it again. And again. And again.

Sure, setbacks are inevitable. By itself, a setback is temporary. Only quitting makes it permanent.

CHAPTER 1

Why sales?

"I am deeply obsessed with the next breath of accomplishment."

—Grant Cardone,
author and entrepreneur

SALES 101 STARTED WHEN I WAS SEVEN

I was fortunate to be returned to my mother after a few months in a foster home. It didn't mean life was going to be simple, though. We moved a lot when I was a kid. Mom and I lived in 20 different apartments before I was 10 years old. It helped me get to know the city, but it made holding onto my prized possessions tough.

Daren and I didn't have a lot of toys as kids, so the few we had, we loved. My G.I. Joe and WWF action figures were holy relics. And the oily palm print I got imprinted on a piece of paper (after slapping Davey Boy Smith, the "British Bulldog," on the shoulder at a WWF event) had massive value to me.

For my brother, it was his Star Wars action figures. I'll never forget Daren's Star Wars collection. It was awesome. He kept nearly every original action figure in a Darth Vader carrying case for safe keeping.

As it turns out, they weren't safe there.

At age seven, I was starting to understand the world around me and I figured there was a considerable market out there for the mint-condition figures. Star Wars was on the lips of every warm-blooded North American male.

One Saturday morning after cartoons, when Daren wasn't around and Mom was busy, I took the Darth Vader carrying case outside to our townhouse complex. I'd seen people come to the door selling cookies before and wondered if I could do the same thing with the Star Wars figures. We always seemed to need extra money for an emergency cab ride or groceries and this seemed like a good way to make some.

I walked door to door around our cul-de-sac, bartering and selling his action figures for pieces of candy, loose change and anything interesting somebody offered up.

When I got back home, I had a serious collection of loot and felt a huge rush of excitement. I was proud of my selling! My brother, on the other hand, was understandably not.*

That surge of pride and sense of accomplishment was a high I've chased ever since. Something magical happened in that moment. The feeling that fed my spirit in the moment

---

* Recently, I tracked down every one of those original Star Wars figures and the Darth Vader carrying case online and gave it to Daren for Christmas. It didn't totally make up for my indiscretion at age seven, but it didn't hurt.

was independence. I am forever, unabashedly, wholeheartedly, deeply obsessed with my next breath of accomplishment. My next deal. My next win. My next taste of independence.

I've had to learn the hard way that these urges can't be satisfied by other means. At times it's been relationships, alcohol, religion and even brushes with the law. All of those have been relatively temporary. Relative, that is, compared to selling. Relative to hustling for a life that's just a little bit better tomorrow.

HUSTLING FOR A BETTER TOMORROW — AND A BIGGER SLURPEE

I learned to hustle early. I knew how to recognize opportunity and I was raised to understand that nothing comes unless you work at it with creativity, consistency and a smile.

I discovered the value of recycling for cash when I was seven. A couple of days of bottle collecting was enough for me to learn precisely how many bottles I needed to bring to the depot to earn enough to buy a big bag of chips. And with two bottles more, I could get the super-sized Slurpee. Sure, it took me an extra two hours to find those bottles, but when I pulled it off, there was that feeling again. The one from when I sold Daren's Star Wars collection: achievement, independence and security tied to nobody's actions but my own.

I wasn't against working to get what I wanted and knew I had to be persistent. Most of hustling is the hard work that comes after you identify an opportunity and follow through on it to achievement.

Eventually the income I received from collecting bottles failed to meet my growing need for spending cash. It wasn't all about Slurpees and candy for me. I had perceived responsibilities that exceeded the norm for an average kid. I always kept enough cash in the mattress to cover a cab ride and night's stay at the motel for Mom, Daren and me.

It was a "just in case" fund. Just in case social workers came knocking again to see if we had "enough." Or just in case a fight with Mom's boyfriend would leave us out on the street in the cold at 3 a.m. When I realized the best person I could have looking out for me was me, I started to crack the code.

I got my first real job when I was 10: delivering flyers and newspapers to hundreds of homes for a few pennies each. It was my first commission job. The more I delivered, the more I made. I liked those odds.

Mom helped me one particularly frigid day. It was −25 degrees Celsius and she bundled me up and joined me to make sure my newspapers were delivered on time. She taught me lessons about responsibility, commitment, work and family simultaneously. She was always there to help.

At the age of 12, I switched from paper delivery to selling pop and chips at the bingo hall on Wednesday evenings. I made $15 a night, plus tips. The secret ingredient to success with that job was simply my smile. There's nothing like an overly polite 12-year-old boy trying to up-sell you on the size of your coffee with a big grin.

I was the king at the local convenience store every following Thursday, buying hot dogs and Slurpees for my buddies and lending a little cash if needed. Although I was good at sharing my profits, I was also good at saving a few dollars for a rainy day and it rained a lot back then.

From the age of 12, I've never been—not for a moment—without a legitimate source of income. In addition to a survival mechanism, this drive to know where my next dollar was coming from was a quality I learned from my mom. I've never known her to not have a job.

I grabbed onto these early experiences of establishing independence with both hands. I went on to get two part-time jobs at 13: working at a hamburger shop after school and dishwashing at a seafood restaurant on the weekend.

By age 15 I had three jobs at once. To me it was just necessity, but to the local CBC radio outlet, it was newsworthy. They even interviewed me about it.

Unfortunately, my three jobs weren't enough. At 15 I was paying my school fees, and buying my own clothes, bus passes and food because I wasn't going home much.

Fortunately, the hamburger joint I worked at was located

right beside a pool hall. Over the course of the two years I worked at the restaurant I became good at pool. So good, in fact, I realized it was a way to make a few bucks.

A guy who worked at the pool hall—we called him Bambino—became a mentor to me. Bambino was unbelievable at pool. He was the only guy in the pool hall who was shorter than me. He taught me the ropes, how to make bank shots, break and how to use my own pool cue.

Bambino also taught me how to hustle, in the more traditional sense of the word.

He did it by hustling me.

I'd watched him play for money from time to time and then one day I asked if he wanted to play me for money. I wasn't nearly as good as him, but I did have my lucky streaks.

Or so I thought.

I ended up losing my entire paycheque to Bambino. All $148 of it. He sat me down and explained the rules of the game. "There are the rules we post on the wall, Dennis; and there are the rules that we don't."

Bambino told me there are times to show off your skills and times to keep them under wraps. In sports, business and life, people generally play to win. But playing fair isn't universal, especially when the stakes are high. In fact, sometimes your opponent will intentionally play to lose to ensure they can get the stakes high enough so that later it's worth playing to win at all costs.

Bambino's rules helped me get very good at the game of pool. Eventually I could turn a few hours at the pool table into a few hundred dollars. I didn't know at the time his rules went way beyond the table. Knowing those rules is integral, especially when you're up against them.

THE UNWRITTEN RULES OF THE HUSTLE

My youth was filled with opportunities to either make money or steal money. I was surrounded by chances to make a bad decision. I needed to pick a side.

One such opportunity make money presented itself when the Olympics came to town in 1988. The streets were filled with people from around the world with money to spend. Apparently there are tons of people who go pin-crazy at every Olympics. There were groups of people wandering around with lanyards around their necks covered with just about every kind of pin you could imagine.

Some pins were more valuable, some were rare and others simply looked cool. My buddy's friend worked for a local television station and had access to panda-shaped pins.

The panda pins we had fell somewhere between cool and valuable, but we determined that in the mass of people there had to be a few who would deem the panda pins to have collector status. We got the pins by the handful, then headed downtown where we'd heard pin collectors would pay up to $100 for a rare pin—it was heaven!

But it didn't come without a little hustle. We were able to dial in on people by opening friendly conversations, building hype by the five of us going from group to group, bidding up the prices whenever someone showed interest.

By the third night of work, we had helped establish our pins as a serious collector's item. These panda pins were worth at least $50 each and we were eventually selling them directly rather than trying to trade up. We would each sell about 10 pins a night, netting a cool $500. It was a serious windfall for me. I didn't realize it was my first taste of commission sales. I was used to making $200 a week peeling potatoes and washing dishes.

The group of us rode the Calgary Tower to the very top and celebrated our pin fortune with a king's feast of unlimited Cokes and fries. We were rich, but it wouldn't last long.

Between washing dishes, hustling pool and trading pins I was making almost $1,000 a month.

Those happy times, where I felt on top of the world, were few and far between as a kid, but I savoured them as best I could. I knew I had to savour them, because I grew up afraid. Afraid of where my family would sleep most nights, afraid of whether or not my family would be taking another trip to the hospital because Mom's boyfriend got out of control again. I was afraid my life was totally different than everyone else's, and that the long-term results of that fact would be devastating.

I used this fear as energy to create a life and routine that would give me independence from the decisions of people whose motives were not my own and who would get in the way of me finding happiness.

A SECRET TO SURVIVING THE STREETS AT 13 AND CLOSING SALES MY WHOLE LIFE

I learned early to keep my eyes open and my mouth shut. It's an excellent lesson for both life and business. They say in sales there's a very important reason we've been given two ears and one mouth. I learned where the lines were drawn and made plans to stay on the right side of the line whenever possible. Even more importantly, I learned when and how to step over the line, without disturbing the peace, to get what I needed.

My family and the people who made up the world around me were my greatest teachers.

I learned what led to jail and what resulted in a reward. I learned what actions made enemies and which words attracted friends. I learned there were certain substances that caused problems and others that fuelled great adventures. I learned how to recognize the difference between a bad person and a person having a bad day. I learned how to avoid danger and when it was appropriate to fight for what was right. I learned most of this simply by paying attention to the dysfunctional yet loving world I lived in.

Zig Ziglar, a motivational speaker who was a big influence on me from early on, once said, "The tougher you are on yourself, the easier life will be on you." Since hearing his words, I've consciously chosen to follow them daily as a universal principle.

Even as a child I understood the principle that things would get easier if I learned from my experiences. Although I didn't like the places I landed when taken from my mom, I didn't resist or complain; I learned to appreciate the pain and use it as fuel to get what I wanted.

Life can ultimately land us in shitty situations. Sometimes we put ourselves there and sometimes it just happens by accident. Either way, it's no good to dwell on what's wrong from a place of defeat. Those of us who want something better can use the rough spots as motivation to get up, get out and shake off the dust on our way to our ultimate goals.

At age 13, I believed that my family could shake off the dust. One day, Mom and I would be out of the fog and into a position where we could head in a new direction without fear. That headspace led me to ditch the pin-trading and look for jobs with steady hours and guaranteed paydays.

By 14, I was out of the house and making enough money to

support myself … kind of. It was getting too unpredictable at Mom's so I couch-surfed and charmed my way into spare bedrooms and onto pull-out couches until my welcome was worn out. Lucky for me, I was good at making friends. I was good at saying the right things and attracting the right types of people. So I wasn't completely homeless.

My favourite place to not be homeless was with my friends whose parents had big houses in nice neighbourhoods. Already used to bouncing around a lot, I learned to get close to people quickly as I scraped together a life of independence. Eventually I realized that while being a dishwasher and cleaning the floors at a hospital were good gigs for a ninth grader, a high schooler needed something better. School fees in high school were more expensive.

I kept my eyes open for a higher-paying job. One day after work, I learned there was a bi-weekly poker game after hours in the restaurant where I washed dishes, hosted by the owner's brother. He'd seen me play pool and I guess it endeared me enough to him that he let me stick around to watch. After several weeks and several games where I was a fly on the wall, I asked if I could join in.

A few hours later there I was: 15 years old, all-in and trying to stare down a grown man at 3 a.m. He was a local business legend. He took one look at me and raised me out of the pot.

I knew I had him beat and all I could hear was Bambino

telling me, "There are the rules we post on the wall, Dennis; and there are the rules that we don't." I used the only tool at my disposal. I cried like the little boy I was. Shit, I was about to lose all the money I had in the world.

Thankfully it worked, and another guy backed me. I ended up winning more than $500 that night. It wasn't pretty, but I had learned another very valuable lesson: no matter how good a hand I may have, there will ultimately be somebody in a position to push me out of the pot, but I can at times get backing. Though I've tended to resist the waterworks in subsequent years, learning to leverage the resources around me and making friends whenever possible has been essential to my growth over the years.

But I didn't always win. In fact, a few months into the school year, I lost two whole paycheques—from the restaurant and the hospital mopping job—at one of the poker games. It seemed I'd hit a bad streak at the same time the school board was sending my mom letters threatening to "take action" if someone didn't pay my school fees. Mom was in no position to help financially; she was already doing everything she could to keep it together for Daren and me. I had nobody left to back me.

At work one day, I stole the cash a table had left to pay their bill.

A few days later when I went in for my evening dishwashing shift, the manager, who had become a good buddy, asked to see me in the back room. He'd noticed the till receipts and table bills weren't matching up. A few hundred dollars had gone missing from one of the biggest bills, he told me.

I stood there with both hands in my pockets and did what I'd done at the poker game. I cried. I also lied. I told him it wasn't me. I sensed from the silence filling the room that night he suspected I was lying, but he couldn't be sure.*

My manager also knew my situation. There had been a few nights I slept at the restaurant and in my friend's car near the restaurant. He let me off with a warning.

I didn't feel like I had a legitimate way to make the life I wanted. I knew I had useful skills, ones that other kids didn't have. But I couldn't figure out just yet how to apply them.

So I tried things. And I tried working hard at those things.

I plugged away at whatever I could to make money. They weren't all sweet gigs, but they were all mostly legitimate. I was a burger flipper, line cook, telephone salesman, dishwasher at almost every restaurant in the area, wedding DJ, ski hill dishwasher and Chuck E. Cheese mascot.

PAYOFF

When I earned myself a driver's licence at age 16, I immediately set my sights on buying a car.

I was eyeing a Volkswagen Beetle with a "for sale" sign in the

---

* When I walked into his shop years later and replayed that day to him, he barely remembered it. I paid him back anyway.

window parked just behind the seafood restaurant. It was $1,500.

Based on the hours I could work outside of school at my current wage, I knew that working 30 days in a row as the dishwasher and potato chipper would earn me enough to buy the car. The restaurant owners, who had become like parents to me, agreed to give me 30 shifts in a row.

On about Day 23, the restaurant received a call from the labour board advising I wasn't allowed to work that much. Given my age and the laws, it was illegal. I got around that by doubling up on my hospital housekeeping shifts instead. I hustled.

I remember scratching a lottery ticket around that same time. At the restaurant, we pooled our money for lottery tickets from the convenience store across the street. I loved the scratch and wins. Worked to the bone, I realized even if I won the lottery, no car I bought with the winnings would feel as good as the car I was about to buy with my next paycheque. I think that's a strength I've never given up on. I'll always bet big on the things that are under my control rather than take a chance on those that aren't.

I didn't win the lottery. I did buy the car with my next paycheque. It felt amazing. It's been a lot of years since I last bought a lottery ticket.

But like all great deals, that beautiful red Volkswagen Beetle was a little too good to be true. I found out really fast about its massive oil leak. It had no working heater. And then there were the holes in the floor. I got in touch with the guy who'd sold it to me and he reminded me the bill of sale said, "Sold as is, where is."

Lesson learned. I did my best to keep the car on the road. Even with no heat and an unusually high oil bill, it was my new-found freedom.

FORGIVENESS

Things were starting to look up in high school. New car. New school. New independence. Best of all, my best friend's mom let me stay with their family.

On our second week in this high school, my best friend Craig and I got into an "altercation" during lunch hour at the convenience store.

What started as a shouting match between me and an older guy who was picking bottles escalated into an all-out brawl that stopped traffic at a major intersection downtown.

Injuries were minor on both sides. They were eclipsed by the media coverage.

That night, sitting back at the house discussing the events of the day with Craig and his mom, we shrugged it off like typical 16-year-old boys.* A few hours later, we were both arrested as part of the police investigation into the brawl.

---

* Years later, I recognized that same man panhandling downtown. I tapped him on the shoulder and explained who I was. He didn't seem to remember me but I apologized for what I'd done as a teenager anyway and put some cash in his cup.

By 2 a.m., though, we were bailed out. I was shocked. I was sure they hadn't tracked down my mom. In a time before everyone had a cellphone in their pocket, I couldn't always reach her on any given day.

It turned out Craig's mom had bailed out both of us. She didn't say a word all the way back home. I was sure she was about to give me a swift kick out the door. When we walked through the door, I was ready to see a suitcase filled with all my worldly possessions. What I found was a freshly made bed and an invitation to stay there permanently.

She made it clear my situation was desperate and both Craig and I were in big trouble. This could be home, but if either of us were ever brought home by the police, it would become home for neither of us. The line had been drawn.

Forgiveness, to me, is a willingness to see past a person's momentary behaviour and offer them the opportunity, direction and support to make different decisions in the future.

Forgiveness is something I have received and experienced in abundance. It doesn't just feel good to get, it feels exceptional to give. I keep that in mind whenever I'm hesitating about calling past clients to uncover problems.

Forgiveness is also about understanding somebody's intention and the deeper circumstances contributing to their behaviour. Simple circumstance can lead to desperate actions despite the best intentions. People who are afraid will often act in random and radical ways.

Believing in forgiveness means I also believe in giving people the chance to explain their actions. I'm not saying all bad behaviour should go unpunished. Not at all. But some actions, despite their consequences, are worth further investigation before I write off a person.

I found my first real sense of normal in that household. I was able to join their family. The police didn't come back to the house, but things weren't easy. Craig and I were eyeballs-deep in trouble and we kept hanging out with a crowd that had no problem finding more.

We were both placed into a new school where we were told it was our last chance at any school in the city. Another clear line in the sand.

The new school was completely different, and so were the affluent, suburban kids who went there. I spent the better part of my first year there wandering the hallways alone and my lunch hours in the bathroom. Craig had made fast friends with the actor crowd and I didn't fit in with his new artsy, scholarly pals. Then I spent weekends partying and drinking with my old friends.

I came really close to getting kicked out of school. I got in a fight with a senior student and ended up in the guidance counsellor's office. She was familiar with my file which, unbeknownst to me, had followed me through my whole school life. There was stuff in there I had no idea existed. For example, a letter I wrote to myself for an assignment in Grade 2. It alluded to my home life. It brought tears to both our eyes.

The counsellor said she would help me make it through high school, but made it clear I needed to help myself.

The line had been drawn.

I owe a lot of my success to the people like my guidance counsellor, Craig's mom and a legal aid lawyer I was given at 13. They all took the time and the risk to get to know me and my story for what it really was instead of judging my book by its cover. They offered forgiveness.

They gave me a hand up versus a handout. Don't get me wrong, I firmly believe there are people in this world who would take that hand up and cut it off in the process. But most of us just need someone to give us an honest opportunity; a chance to catch our breath and get a good night's sleep. Access to a positive role model and the chance to learn from best practices goes a long way.

In this same way, now that I'm grown up, I'm careful not to write people off based on snap judgements.

It doesn't always work out. I have been wrong. I have been let down and I have been taken advantage of. However, whenever it's possible I investigate further. I have had people steal from me directly and I still do business with them.

I've gotten to know young people who have committed crimes and were labelled troublemakers. Those same people are now leading some of the most important, life-changing organizations I'm connected to.

We have to let people be many different things on their way to their highest good. Not all those things will look good and some of them won't be good. Great relationships happen because we are willing to run the marathon with the people around us.

These types of people, those who need a second chance, are all around us. Take a look at the business leaders, game changers and pioneers in our world. People like Virgin Group's Richard Branson, rapper and producer Jay Z, business superstar Martha Stewart, or former U.S. president Bill Clinton. Shit happens and sometimes we step in it. All those people, at some point in their stories, ultimately fell on tough times, dark times and times of compromise. They emerged stronger and clear-headed, and became massive contributors to the world we live in because of their efforts. Something or someone appeared and provided those people a second chance to succeed.

Often, the path to a life of misfortune can be triggered by a simple accident. Being in the wrong place at the wrong time or being unable to make the right decision due to frame of mind, inexperience or pressure.

Someone isn't a bad person, or even a lost cause, until the consequences of their actions set them down the path of no return. Given the chance to do it all over again, some of these people will make a different decision. Those are the people I await to help because I was one of them.

Young people in particular live with the unfortunate reality of no personal experience and sometimes a severe lack of positive role models and teachers along the way. I was that person. I've walked the very fine line between stealing and hustling, lying and negotiating. I've seen the other side of bars in a cage and also stood on stage being handed a trophy.

Thankfully I got caught early. I had people sit me down and explain consequences. I learned the rules, written and unwritten. I knew what it was like to be separated from the people I loved.

I also learned that just because I did bad things, didn't mean I had to be stuck being a bad kid. It was an important distinction. It meant I was ultimately responsible for all of my decisions. I saw first-hand what happens when you cross the line deliberately. I saw potential for change.

I have stepped over the line and been invited back. If you're not somebody who walks the line then you can be somebody who keeps an eye out for those who do and do your best to help them.

OPEN WIDE AND SAY 'AWE'

One night in high school, shortly after meeting my guidance counsellor, I went out partying very late. It wasn't a good night. After I stumbled back into my basement bedroom at Craig's house, I found my hand on a Bible. I opened it up in search of something and found a simple verse that for me may as well have been the entire Bible summed up.

"Just as you swallowed up my people on my holy mountain, so you and the surrounding nations will swallow the punishment I pour out on you. Yes, all you nations will drink and stagger and disappear from history.

"But Jerusalem will become a refuge for those who escape; it will be a holy place. And the people of Israel will come back to reclaim their inheritance." (Obadiah 1:16-17)

I'd never been to church in my life at that point, but the verse resonated.

The next day I woke up with a hangover and a new sense of who I was and where I wanted to go. I can't say it actually came to fruition overnight, or the next week or even that year. But something did happen that first night; I made a conscious choice to set my sights forward rather than behind me or on others.

That's part of how I ended up in Bible college. The other part was shortly after high school, I had my heart broken by the girl I thought I would marry. A few weeks after she unexpectedly decided we needed time apart, she was engaged.

She said it was a "God thing." A spiritual thing. Something I "wouldn't be able to understand." I never have been able to understand it. At the time, it sent me on a quest to try.

So I enrolled in Bible college. I was just really curious. Most people I met there said they were "called" to be there, whatever that meant. I didn't feel any calling.

Bible college was short-lived, but it led me to work with youth on a bunch of levels. I nearly made that a career, but it was quickly clear the needs in that area exceeded the resources available. I wanted to become someone who could help provide the resources.

Ministry work combined with dishwashing didn't seem like the brightest path to get me where I wanted to go either financially or spiritually.

My search continued for a career I could sink my teeth into. I still had bills to pay and dreams that were starting to become pretty big. The best I could do was become a dental technician.

LUCK COMES FROM HARD WORK, PREPARATION AND OPPORTUNITY

Getting into the dental industry didn't happen by accident. Like most of the opportunities I've been given, when it came to the dental industry, somebody opened the door for me and

I pried it the rest of the way open to take a long look at what I could accomplish in there. There was a lot of mundanity in the work, but it meant I got to tap into the knowledge of the people around me and learn valuable lessons that weren't directly tied to the job. It stoked my fires further for the future.

My friend Owen was working in the model room of a dental lab. His primary job was making molds for dentures, including casting the metal frames that would eventually be used to make a custom-fitting piece for somebody's teeth. He moved up the ladder quickly there and invited me to follow.

We both worked incredibly hard and as consistently as possible to make the best of the opportunity. I eventually applied for a few positions outside of the lab where I worked with Owen and that's what led to my big break.

I was invited back for a second interview at one lab. I would have to sit a two-hour practical exam with the rest of the interviewees. We were each given a large block of clay, some carving tools, measuring instruments and specific measurements to reproduce. This was a job that would ultimately result in making dentures for people; precision mattered.

Although I had done fairly well in the plaster room at my first dental lab, I'd never worked on the technical side at this level. Knowing I'd need to go above and beyond to make an impression, I put in an extra 60 minutes after all the other job candidates had finished. I measured carefully and carved every nook and cranny as precisely as I could to ensure it was exactly what they were asking for. When I walked out of the room I was sure I'd created a perfect model.

I learned later that I'd strayed far away from what they were looking for.

Oops.

It was still good news for me, though. The dental lab co-owner Colin appreciated the extra time I put in, and my creative approach to problem-solving, despite half-wondering if I was stoned while doing the exam. (I wasn't.)

They hired me based on the potential they saw and the energy I brought into the room with me.

It turned out that extra hour of carving clay into the shape of bicuspids and molars led to one of the most influential relationships of my life. Colin was a bit of a square peg in the dental industry. He's creative, intuitive and a high-level-thinking entrepreneur.

Colin turned into a mentor for me. On breaks we talked philosophy, religion, goals and the possibilities that existed for us in the world. We eventually talked each other out of a job in the dental industry. Between the books on tape I listened to on my Walkman while working in the lab and the one-on-one talks with Colin outside of it, my desire to find the next great thing for me was stoked.

But before I left the dental industry, another mentor rubbed off on me. My supervisor Todd was one of the hardest workers I'd ever met. He loved to come to work super early, work hard all day and then leave in time to get a couple of hours of fishing in before getting back to his family.

He invited me to take part in a similar schedule. I'd never been an early riser and had rarely fished. However, starting the day a bit early to leave early seemed to make sense, so I joined him. He set me up on some basic fishing gear, gave me a bit of instruction and boom—I caught my first fish. I was hooked. Not so much on fishing, but on the ability to control and manipulate my schedule to get an extraordinary amount of work done before the busyness of the rest of the lab set in, then fit in a few hours of recreational freedom to fish, think and enjoy the outdoors.

What I didn't expect was the chance to get in touch with my inner spirit while walking along rivers or sitting on lakes during those years. Fishing can bring about an almost meditative state.

Although the dental industry didn't have a whole lot to teach me directly, the people in it sure did. It's always been important to me to do whatever job is in front of me with 110% of my effort, for as long as required until something better is absolutely in place in front of me.

I can honestly say I've never not made the very best of

whatever job or situation I was in despite how ambitious I may have been relative to the size of the job.

Eventually, four years into the dental industry I decided punching a clock was a little too boring. I think I was so used to a lack of consistency that I couldn't adjust comfortably to someone else's routine.

The Star Wars salesman, Chuck E. Cheese mascot and dental technician in me all knew I was capable of something greater. Something that was really me.

I reached out to opportunities as I came across them and kept my eyes wide open in search of better. Vacuum cleaner sales, vitamin sales, alarm sales and just about anything else in sales. I was attracted to the offer of seemingly unlimited potential to earn cash based on my energy and talent. All along the way, I kept my foot on first base for as long as possible before daring to steal second. I was never in unknown territory regarding where my cash would come from.

The early shift in the dental industry had allowed me to find time to go to the gym. It was in this recreational activity that I found my next big break. One day at the gym I was chatting with a man I knew. He seemed to have a comfortable life; he drove a nice car and had the time to work out. I wondered what his secret sauce was. He told me he was in the health and wellness business specializing in cookware sales. He told me he'd share the opportunity with me over a dinner.

I learned at dinner that he was about my age, 26, and had already been selling cookware for a decade. The guy who got his boss into it was Zig Ziglar, that motivational speaker I listened to a ton on my headphones in the dental lab. I couldn't disguise my interest.

After an hour of talking, seeing his show and hearing about how Zig had started his career the same way, I came home with an expensive set of pots and pans (which I bought through a finance company at an almost-illegal interest rate) and a renewed hunger for the art of selling.

Pots and pans taught me a ton. Cold-calling, dinner shows, trade shows and thousands of miles on the road. It was the greatest single thing I did for my career by that point.

Easy? No. Worth it? Absolutely.

CASE STUDY: ABOVE AND BEYOND

When I sold pots and pans, every potential client received a dinner show from yours truly. That meant I hauled my pots and pans, plus food, into their kitchen and cooked for them. The dinner presented an opportunity to learn about their life so that on the fly, I could present the product so it made sense for their lifestyle.

My presentation was aimed at asking questions that

triggered responses so I could identify which of four areas were most important to the prospect:

1. The price.
2. Saving money and time.
3. Health and wellness for potential client and their family.
4. Quality and warranty.

Getting to know people can be rewarding without the sale, and I've learned relationships can head in many directions. But to go in any direction, a relationship has to start somewhere. There were times when I would stay after a dinner show or return for a visit to chat, have drinks and even dinner (cooked by them that time) without ever having made the sale initially. I did it not only because I got to know and like and even learn from these people, but also because I understood that sales—whether pots and pans or houses—is about the marathon.

GOOD OLD-FASHIONED HUSTLE

As a pots and pan salesman I did dinner shows in a lot of different places around our province and country. I often travelled with the salesman who recruited me as a travelling roadshow. We were cooking guys who knocked on the door wearing aprons.

The process we went through to book our sales dinners was good old-fashioned hustle. There were no shortcuts to that one.

We would do trade shows at different venues and collect

a few hundred names at each. Every person who entered our draw was a winner. Everyone won a dinner show, compliments of me showing up at their home with a suitcase full of cookware and a cooler of food.

At the end of a trade show weekend I'd take the hundreds of leads and break them down into different categories. People I could remember (warm leads); owners of the product; business owners; and finally, the "maybe later" pile. Then I would call each person with my very solid script congratulating them on the eight-course meal they'd won. It was absolutely free, fully catered, and included prep and all the clean-up. All they had to do was invite a few friends and supply any booze. Not a bad deal. My script was very specific, but sounded organic at the same time.

The goal for me as the salesman was, as it should always be, to get a date on the calendar. Free food for a date on the calendar. That was all. Once the date was booked over the phone, we would start the qualifying process in a second call. Is this person actually interested in my product? Too many organizations and sales people make the barrier to entry too high. They qualify right up front and dig for personal information to determine if it will be a "waste of time" for them. I had to know if the person on the other end of the phone was a vegetarian before I showed up to talk about benefits of cooking roast beef. Make sure you're at least speaking the same language as your clients.

You have to give before you can get. This is huge. Regardless if it's pots and pans or it's selling real estate, we always give something significant before we ask for anything. Back then it was a free dinner and a date on the calendar, then we would qualify. Nobody was a waste of my time because I always put in the effort to know if they were a prospective client. Today in real estate, my team books appointments and offers to show properties any time that works for the client. Then we qualify.

Our closing rate for booking women was higher than that of men. It was nothing to do with me in an apron, believe me. The biggest challenge wasn't actually booking the date, it was getting the date to stick. You can only imagine how many women we would speak to and put a date on the calendar for a free dinner but when we went to confirm the appointment, her husband answered the phone. He had a different set of questions and qualifying criteria. The guys were more skeptical to say the least.

A few dozen calls would result in two or three dates which resulted in one or two actual dinners. Every call required hustle.

MY BIGGEST DINNER EVER

One of the more memorable pots and pans calls I landed was a very excited woman who answered the phone with complete interest. It was a welcome change from the skepticism that typically made the first minute of conversation the most difficult.

When I explained she'd won a free dinner show for her, her family and as many friends as she could invite, I felt her hug me through the phone.

We set a date and she promised to call back with a confirmation on the number of guests.

When I got her next call, she said there would be 60 people at dinner. I thought for sure she was joking. Normally we cooked for between five and 10 people. Fifteen max.

After a little more digging I learned the dinner would be at a Hutterite colony a few hours outside the city. At this particular colony, the women did the cooking. The men would be out working while we were doing the dinner show.

The woman on the phone advised me there would be about 30 women in attendance and the men would join after dark for the food.

This didn't fit our business plan. I insisted both the men and women be there for the whole show because it was unlikely a big purchase for a few thousand dollars would be made by only one party. A good general rule in sales is to know who the decision-makers are and ensure they're in attendance for the sales presentation.

She was unwilling to budge, so, against the advice of my colleagues and boss at the shop, I went ahead with the dinner. Everyone told me I was nuts.

The woman on the other end of the phone assured me that if they were interested in a purchase, they would be able to make a quick decision based on the input of the women in attendance.

I decided to give before I got. We booked the dinner.

I rounded up an assistant who was a colleague in the business and we headed to the colony to cook our biggest dinner show ever.

It was a total gong show.

I was a pretty good cook at this point but I wasn't an entire catering company. With yours truly at the helm, we burned the cake, undercooked the chicken, overcooked the roast beef and ran out of potatoes.

There was very little selling happening but a whole lot of entertaining. Just as planned, the men joined in just after dark. They came in and polished off every ounce of food remaining. Then they asked us to make more dinner. And a couple more cakes to top things off ("Not burned please."). Although I had run out of supplies, they had plenty in store. I've never seen grown men eat so many potatoes.

The dinner stretched late into the evening. Despite the food being below average, they wanted to spend a considerable amount of time talking about the quality of the pots and pans, the service we would provide after the sale and, most important to them, the lifetime warranty offered on each item.

We all got along well and although there was no sale to be had that night it was without a doubt my most memorable dinner to date.

Before we left, we were invited down to the head of the colony's house so our host Eli could pour us a drink and make us a sandwich. It was here I learned that they made their own bologna, cheese and some very good white wine. We ate, drank and laughed even later into the evening.

At about 4 a.m. Eli invited us to head down to the big barn for an after-party with all of the young people. I thought we should go check it out, but my colleague informed me there was no way in hell he was getting out of our vehicle to dance on a stomach full of bologna. So we did a U-turn and headed back to town.

There was no closing that night. But, like a lot of my dates when I was young, there was a request that I follow up in a few days.

I called Eli, after a couple days had passed, from a pay phone at school. I was so broke I couldn't afford my cellphone bill. On top of that, I had a truck payment coming up.

When Eli answered, he was elated to hear from me. We small-talked for a few minutes and then he told me he would like to place an order. I was making notes as he talked and it dawned on me: the order he was placing was the single biggest order I had placed in my entire career.

My average commission at that time for a dinner show was

approximately $1,000. The order he placed with me was approximately $5,000. Even better, I had no fear of credit falling through because he wanted to pay cash.

Shit, I thought I was ready to retire. I went back out to the colony and spent a full afternoon with him and the rest of his team. We laughed and ate bologna sandwiches and I set them up with their cookware.

Eli still calls me whenever he's in town.

THERE ARE NO SHORTCUTS TO A GOOD RELATIONSHIP

Everyone prefers to do business with someone they know and like. And when they don't get to, they wish they were.

I can't tell you how many times a seemingly casual interaction with a stranger at a coffee shop or party has led to a relationship that turns into a request for sales. I'm regularly approached by a friend-of-a-friend-of-a-friend referred by someone I met socially who found me "memorable."

This isn't because I'm anything special or that I say smart things or wear unforgettable outfits. It's simply because I learned what Dale Carnegie taught a long time ago: "The best way to be interesting is to be interested." I strongly believe that no matter how you do it, to be successful in sales it is essential to:

○ Take the time to build relationships face-to-face.

- Keep your ears wide open.
- Ask good questions and be interested in the answers.

FROM POTS AND PANS TO THE WHOLE HOUSE

In my final year of college, a lot of factors coalesced at once that led me into real estate. I was selling pots and pans on the days I wasn't in class and making cold calls between classes. I was good at sales, but I knew I didn't want to sell pots and pans forever.

In the back of my mind was the memory of a real estate agent I'd been able to watch from afar: my high school girl-friend's dad. Then, when my new wife and I were loaned the down payment to buy a house, a real estate agent friend of ours helped us to find and buy one that was right for us.

Seeing what those two real estate guys did, how they did it and how successful they were at it gave me an undeniable confidence that I could do it too. I wanted to sell real estate.

Naïve, desperate and determined was the perfect recipe.

It seemed like a logical transition. Selling pots and pans involved a lot of time on the phone, plenty of time in the car and ultimately meeting people in their homes, cooking dinner for them and then sitting down at their kitchen table at the end of an evening to discuss their priorities and how my product may best assist them to achieve what was important to them.

I went from being in people's houses and selling them

cookware to being in people's houses and ultimately selling them the whole house. I was already pretty good at the former. How much harder could the latter be?

The critical window with the pots and pans business was 10 days after signing the paperwork. Customers had 10 days to cancel the order if things weren't working out or they weren't satisfied for any reason. Nurturing the client during these 10 days was critical.

Some people chose to ignore their client after the sale and hope for the best. I wasn't one of those salesmen and preferred phone calls, meetings and as much service and support as possible. This would serve me well in my transition to real estate.

Many of my initial clients in the real estate business came directly from my pots and pans business. I cared for and nurtured every single one of the relationships and carried many of them over with me. I have sold houses for individuals who never bought pots and pans, but did eat the free food I cooked them with my pots and pans.

One of the families I called to see how things were going let me know that they hadn't had a chance to unpack their cookware yet. The husband told me he had been transferred to a new job unexpectedly and said they would be moving within the next few weeks.

I quickly put on my real estate agent hat and asked if I could come out and do an evaluation of his home to see how I might be able to help him. He agreed. I remember being so nervous that I left the listing appointment having sweat so much I looked like I'd peed through the back of my pants.

It was weird for me to have that nervous reaction, though. I'd already sold to him before. I knew his story and was sure he'd left our previous encounter feeling he got a good deal.

The reality was, I didn't need to sweat through my pants. I was going to get that listing. It was a done deal when I called about the pots and pans. It was an act that showed I cared about him beyond the initial sale at a serendipitous time when he happened to be looking for someone to trust with an even bigger purchase. Once you are in their hearts, you have a real connection. At that point, it's not about paperwork and paycheques. It's about a human connection.

I've never looked back. I experienced exponential growth personally, professionally and financially from my earliest days hawking Chewbacca door to door. Each experience has led to the next in pursuit of better.

Looking back, I've noticed one of the secrets to my learning is that I've always made an effort to start conversations, whether it's picking up the phone or walking up to a person I'm curious about. Simply starting conversations led me to what was next when I moved into real estate and it continues to make things happen for me today.

Hard work, caring about every client, the pursuit of better and at the same time doing the best with what I have has always led to good things. This has been proven in the past and I believe it will be my future as well.

CHAPTER 2

The art of negotiation

"Know the rules well, so you can break them effectively."

–Dalai Lama XIV

UNDERSTAND THE OPTIONS

I am a very good negotiator.

I have learned what it takes to win, and I know the best way to do it so that everyone has a reason to smile at the end. I want everyone to be treated fairly at the end of a negotiation. To get to "fair," you have to ask for as much as you can.

But to know what to ask for and the best way to ask for it, you need to understand the rules.

Rules to me are like signposts. They're intended to point us in the right direction and keep us safe and playing nice. However they're just rules—not laws—and sometimes rules are bent or broken.

To be clear, when I say rules, I'm not talking about laws. Rules are the unwritten cultural norms and societal expectations that we have amongst each other. Be kind, be generous, be respectful, be honest. When you break one of those rules, there are social consequences.

Laws, on the other hand, result in serious penalties when they're broken. However, there are times where just about everyone you know has pushed the limit of a law. For example, speeding into oncoming traffic to safely pass a slow-moving vehicle on the highway is still living within the law. Sometimes it just has to happen to get to where you're going.

A good rule is that you shouldn't be rude to people whom you meet on the street. The law says you can't punch them in the face.

Please understand that I'm not about to say you should go around breaking social rules as a salesperson, but you should learn to occasionally push their limits to the very edge. In sales, it can be costly and frustrating to make sure (or to assume) everyone follows all the rules—is telling you the whole truth, is giving you the best deal possible—all the time. There are people whose job it is to ensure lines aren't crossed, and it is a job that will never fully be complete.

Strict adherence to rules can be crippling for an entrepreneur looking to get a deal done. Day-to-day we have to navigate rules that aren't especially clear.

Some rules are interpretive. "No shirt, no shoes, no service," for example. At what point does casual footwear cease being a "shoe"? Are flip-flops all right? Is a tank top a "shirt" on a woman but not on a man? How about those signs that say, "You must shower before entering the pool"? Is it a quick rinse or a scrub-down?

And many rules are cultural, like eating halal or how to use your car's horn. In some countries, everyone honks through their whole commute, but elsewhere it's seen as obnoxious and in some countries it can get you a ticket.

In some places, it's fine to wear no clothes on a beach. Elsewhere, you needn't use cutlery during your meal.

There are rules you can read on the wall and there are rules you can't read. At the pool hall when I was learning the ropes from Bambino, there were written rules against foul language, no outside food and drink, no tilting the video games or hitting the cues on the pool table. The unwritten rule was that you shouldn't take advantage of players with weaker skills than you.

We've all seen the rule that says, "All staff must wash hands before returning to work." Here's hoping that one is never compromised.

Some rules you have to learn while others you should trust experts to navigate for you. The unwritten rules of negotiation include being respectful and courteous, tactful and careful. It's expected you're not going to steal information. It's also expected that you'll be bluffing. While you're bluffing, the unwritten rules are that you respect your opponent. If you don't, you can't expect the negotiation to go very far.

The written rules of negotiation fall into the area of the law.

That's when experts step in: contracts, legal implications of disclosure and non-disclosure. These written rules vary based on the industry or the product at the centre of the negotiation.

The reality is everybody pushes the limits of rules at times and those who try desperately to keep people from doing so are going to be left chasing their tails. It's been said that wisdom is the ability to know when to keep the rules and when to create exceptions.

When I was seven, I stole something. It was a Joe Louis pastry from a convenience store. Mom and I had just moved to a new neighbourhood. One Saturday morning I woke up before her and I was hungry. Really hungry. I'd remembered seeing the convenience store from the car the day before so I beelined it there in my little brown Cougar boots.

I made nice with the man at the till before I lifted the Joe Louis. I ate it on the walk home. Or at least, what I thought would be the walk home. I walked past the new apartment and got totally lost. If you believe in this sort of thing, you might say it was my first brush with karma. I was scared and lucky for me a nice neighbour picked me up and helped me find my house.

I'm not proud of that moment at age seven, but I wouldn't necessarily change it. I stole the Joe Louis because I was hungry. I was a little kid, we'd moved out of the neighbourhood I used to know and felt I had no other option to feed myself.

I have a different sense of this event today and I am

keenly aware that other options, like the food bank, do exist. Unfortunately, at seven years old I couldn't think of any. Not on that Saturday morning anyway.

I believe one of the realities in the world is that desperate people take desperate measures because they are unaware of other options in the moment. Do your best to understand the options before you bend any rules.

THE 'RULES' YOU CAN BEND

Let me put it to you this way: would you jaywalk to save a puppy about to be run over by a bus?

What about if you had no change and couldn't pay to park in front of the hospital where you needed to pick up a sick relative? Would you park anyway? Would you speed if it meant helping someone in need? What about if you just needed to get somewhere quickly and thought you could get there safely even if you sped? What about answering an important call while driving?

My guess is most people would say yes to most of these questions. Yet, if asked whether they consider themselves law-abiding citizens they would still, truthfully, say they were. Some of these are extremes. But they need to be, because it's only when we wrestle with the edges, the extreme and far-reaching dilemmas of life, that we can ultimately land somewhere in the middle.

When negotiating, there are some cases where the rules

may be tested. I can recognize when it is happening and how to work with it to put my client in the best position possible in the negotiation. That's what a negotiation is about—the bending, dodging and weaving through the gauntlet aimed at achieving a particular outcome. Sure, I wish it wasn't like this, but I'm convinced that most of life (and real estate in particular) is about this delicate navigation.

We all bend the social rules. Whether it's jaywalking or closing a sale, we all navigate the intersection with the same objective in mind: get to the other side and make sure no one gets hurt.

In my opinion, most of the people who are against testing the boundaries feel that way because of fear or a lack of experience much more than 100% conviction to the rules. Pure conviction to rules is a very rare attribute. People's answers to whether or not they would do something anti-social is usually influenced by whether or not they will be caught; as often it's the getting caught that will hurt them or others.

Andrew Wiederhorn, the owner of Fatburger, spent 14 months in a federal prison prior to growing Fatburger to some seriously fat profits. Knowing this doesn't stop me from eating hamburgers there, nor does it stop me from admiring him for all he has accomplished, both pre- and post-prison. Quite the opposite in fact.

Because he has been on the wrong side of prosecution after growing profits the wrong way, he is now one of the best people to have in charge of growing a company the right way. He gets where the lines are now because at some point he didn't get it and it cost him dearly.

I understand that some people believe there's no grey area when it comes to rules and that any action outside the perceived boundaries of fair practice is wrong. To those people I say: I commend their convictions and wish them the very best of luck, which they'll need if they ever come across me in a competitive bid.

NEGOTIATING LEADS TO DISCOMFORT

Humans are for the most part selfish and will instinctively do what's best for themselves. This is how we survive, but it's not always a comfortable place to be.

When it comes to negotiating, those who find the process of asking for what they want to be nerve-wracking often hire an expert to navigate the conversation gauntlet so they don't have to.

Not everybody knows there's a difference between rules and laws. It's a line that we need to be aware of or it will trip us up. Lawyers do this all the time when they write up a contract for a client that is completely legal, but treats one party much more nicely than another.

For example, I was on a plane with my wife recently and we were sitting next to a woman who shared one of her real estate experiences with us. She had been approached by someone who wanted to buy a piece of her land. He played nice—following the social rules—all the way through the initial negotiation and then said he'd have his lawyer draft something to move the sale along.

As it turned out, this contract she signed put her at a serious disadvantage to this supposedly nice guy. She was playing by the social rules of being kind and honest. He was playing the legal procedures to win at his own game. She didn't understand where the social rules left off and the negotiation began.

Rarely in sales do all parties place the same value on the same items. Negotiations are about crafting outcomes to suit the interests of all parties. I'm all about crafting. I've done it my whole life. But let's be clear: there's a difference between crafting and lying. Good negotiators don't lie. They organize how they tell the truth so relevant benefits or risks are emphasized based on their client's unique interests. Lying is making a calculated decision to suppress some or all of a truth.

I'm not OK with lying. For me, lying is saying something that has no chance of being true. But crafting the truth is something we all do all the time, whether consciously or not. Why? Because we need to make decisions about how we shape our communication. We choose to list certain factors over others. We choose phrases that have persuasive value. The best we can do is admit this happens so we can become conscious of it— and make sure we are acting in the interests of all involved.

I choose to be comfortable with crafting when it means I am guiding a person's thinking to accept a truth they haven't considered yet. I am OK with persuading as well, because that is how we all arrive at our decisions.

Another example is divorce attorneys. When it's an acrimonious split, both divorce lawyers are usually crafting the truth and hiding the reality of one spouse's position over the other in order to get their client the best possible outcome. Our legal system is built on the premise that two experts each focusing on their client's best interests is the best way to arrive at a solution. It's not a tea party; it's a negotiation.

In a negotiation I may be required to stress some parts of a truth more than others to help a client see what they may be missing. I need to advocate for my client, even if that means using persuasive language. I'm not making the decision for them, and I will not withhold information to cook the outcome. But I will try to help my client see a decision in ways that help them make a strong choice, rather than get paralyzed by big decisions. I ensure this is always done in their best interest.

For example, a real estate listing may state the seller's requested possession date is 60 days. I don't know if that listing is that way because it's truly a requirement or because the listing agent is aiming for a particular outcome. So, even though my client is OK with 60 days, we may put in an offer asking for possession in 15 days. In the negotiation, that puts the onus on the other party to lower the price to convince us to accept the 60 days. They have to decide between the monetary value and the value of a 60-day possession.

That's crafting. Like it or not, it happens.

It's like when you're shopping and you see an item that's apparently for sale a few bucks below the normal price. Yet, when you peel back the flashy sale price sticker, you see the same price underneath. That's crafting too.

There is a procedure to negotiation—like a dance. And it takes a certain number of moves to arrive at a firm position. Sometimes the entire purpose for a move is just to take up space. It's there because a move had to be made. This is the art of negotiation. Each move gives shape to the whole, and the whole is ideally a great outcome for all involved.

And remember, for every great dance, somebody has to be the lead. For a negotiation I suggest you either take the lead or find a great partner.

Anyone who wishes to be successful in sales must be comfortable with the art of negotiation. Note: I'm referring to negotiating and crafting when it comes to sales specifically. I'm not giving marriage advice or talking about raising children. That also involves an element of sales, but is content for a totally different book. For now, we're talking about negotiating deals that involve hundreds of thousands and sometimes millions of dollars. The stakes are high and we need to be aware.

Let me go one step further. I believe those who are the most successful in business, and even in life, are those who know when and how to push the rules. High performance and strong outcomes happen at the edge. Innovation happens at the edge. The intention isn't to break the rules, but to find new possibilities. It requires a mind that is able to see things differently, and take risks. Our motivation as negotiators, though, must always be the common good, and we should never disregard the rules or seek to break them.

I do not believe that testing the rules is a sign of weak character, but rather a sign of strong character. I am completely honest about when and why I would work to craft the truth. I believe my negotiations are in line with both what my client ultimately needs and the social rules. I'm fair, I'm kind and I don't litter.

PRICE VERSUS VALUE

Call it bluffing, posturing or feinting, all this means is, there is a procedure to negotiation. It is a dance. There are moves made. Some more sincere than others. All the moves are an attempt to find a meaningful middle ground acceptable to both parties. It's not possible to find that middle ground without the dance.

For some, it can be difficult to see whether these moves are truthful or not. It's better to think of the moves of negotiation as "explorations." They are "forays in the direction of a preferable middle ground." Almost like thinking out loud.

For a person of morals, it can be hard to negotiate with a client without walking the fine line between total truth and tall tale. At the end of a meeting with a potential client, or in any sales transaction, the customer only ever wants you to assure them of one thing: You can get them the value they want at the price they need.

They may think they want the product they "need" at the price they "need," but this is where the art of negotiation fills the gap. If I focus on the value instead of the price, I can find a way to make them happy. My friend Dan Roscoe, a talented cellphone plan salesman when I first met him, put it well when he said, "Everyone seems to know the price these days, but few actually know the value."

Exceptional salespeople help establish value, and from there they can work out the price. The art of negotiation attempts to accomplish one of two things:

1. Reach an agreement or compromise through discussions.

2. Find a way over an obstacle or through a difficult path.

Both these definitions apply to what I do as a real estate agent every day with both buyers and sellers.

While I would never promise something I couldn't deliver, I often use the art of negotiation as a way to help clients understand the value of the sale or purchase rather than focusing on the often rigid price.

For example, I regularly hear a seller or buyer tell me their "as low/high as I'll go" price, in their non-negotiable tone of voice early on in our sales discussion. They think they only care about money, but in fact every sale and every purchase is about a lifestyle. It's about how the intended transaction will ultimately affect a person's lifestyle. If we as salespeople can find this out then we will make the sale.

Think about the last new smartphone you bought. What mattered more: the price or the impact it would have on your life?

You don't need a million dollars if you already have everything money can buy. In the same way, through negotiations we're able to convince people other things besides cash can contribute to the value of a sale.

CASE STUDY: WORTH MORE THAN A MILLION

After several years of talking and negotiation, I finally sat down for lunch with a real estate person about me buying part of his business. The years-long negotiation came to a pivotal point over this lunch. I went into lunch expecting another negotiation but I really wanted a conclusion.

The moment came when he said to me, "Let's just say I sell

you half of my business for $1 million. What does it really get me? I don't really need another million dollars. What's a few more zeros in the bank account?"

"Great question," I said. Then I sat back and smiled because I knew I had finally figured out this one.

You see, he was seeing this undertaking as a sale while I was viewing it as a partnership. He was seeing it as giving up something in return for something he already had enough of.

I said: "You're totally right. If it's just about adding $1 million more to your bank account then you probably don't need to sell me half the business.

"But look at it this way. This isn't like selling your last property." (He is a very savvy real estate person who has bought and sold a ton of property.)

"The difference there is you give them the house and they give you a bag full of cash and everyone goes their separate ways," I said. "I'm going to be handing you $1 million and I am coming with it. Fortunately for you, I will now be a full-time part of your world. All of my energy, ideas, marketing expertise and my track record, are going to be fuel in your gas tank. Kind of like a Tesla: unlimited for as long as you own the vehicle. I'm the vehicle and I'm adding power to your empire. You're not selling, you are partnering."

He smiled and said, "Put an offer on paper."

If I was playing by my usual rules of negotiating—stop talking when you have the deal—I would've stopped there and waited for a response but I had just a little more to give him. I broke my own rule. I next asked him, "How old are you?" He told me he was 55.

"Wow," I said. "And you've done so much. I'm not even 40. Remember what it was like when you were 40? Remember how excited and full of piss and vinegar you were? How you were ready to change the world? I'm there now and I want to change our worlds together.

"You should be on a golf course full time in a few years and able to make more money than ever before without losing all the momentum you've built. I'm confident I can help you get there." Then I sat back and took a sip of my drink and smiled back at him.

We finished the meeting with an agreement to construct a business plan and pursue the option further.

At first, he'd stumped me when he asked the question about the $1 million. If a sale is just about exchanging money for a product without any other conversation, emotion or value being conveyed, it's a difficult negotiation.

It's kind of like buying Apple products. The price is the price and there actually isn't a negotiation to be had. Not at the till anyway. The negotiation that happens is the one you have with yourself or your business partners in regards to why everyone on the team needs an iPhone, regardless of the price, because the value is there.

There is ultimately a negotiation involved with every purchase even when we don't think there is. Even the very expensive root canal I had was aimed at solving a massive problem with pain I was having. In that case, after several years of negotiating with myself and tolerating the pain relative to paying the price, I booked the root canal.

That tooth negotiation only ended after I had a candid conversation with a dental specialist who broke it down simply: "You're young and you can either live the rest of your life with or without the hindrance of a bad tooth. Your choice."

I choose less hindrance whenever possible.

The dental work impacted my life in a massive way. I paid them in full with gratitude and delivered a gift basket at the end of it. I never negotiated for a discount as the value I received was worth the price.

Sales needs to involve emotions so people can understand the true value of all the parts of the transaction.

Finding out what a person really values is all about asking the right questions. But knowing what they really value even when they can't necessarily articulate it—that's the art of negotiation. I agree to their price, but then I negotiate within the details to create more value in the sale.

When I am negotiating, I begin with the end in mind. This works as long as I have taken the time to understand a client's end and believe in their end. This is essential for making everyone feel like they've won at the end of the negotiation.

Instead of asking, "What will you pay or won't you pay," it's about asking, "What will happen if you do pay or don't pay a certain amount?" Ask what effect the purchase or lack of purchase will have on their life's plans.

Getting to the "What happens if you do or don't" is essential.

The bottom line is that I will strive to get the value my client needs, not necessarily the exact dollar amount. They get enough value that at the end of the day, when all parties sign off on the deal, each party truly believes—correctly—that they have pulled off something great.

NEGOTIATING IS A BLOOD SPORT

When we humans set our minds on something specific, people will beg, borrow, steal, lie or fight until they get it.

A more socially acceptable way of looking at this struggle is to see every transaction, be it paid for or free of charge, as an act of negotiating.

This concept is easy to understand in countries like Mexico where prices are rarely set in stone and bartering dictates the final sale, but negotiating is part of every culture. Even here in North America, the act of negotiation is embedded in the fabric of everything we do. Mortgages, credit cards, job offers, relationships, traffic court, project due dates—we all negotiate every day whether we know it or not.

Rarely is the outcome of a negotiation a pure win-win and if you think it is, or are oblivious to your ability to influence the result, chances are you'll be on the losing end.

Sometimes, the very people who are successful at negotiating for that fake silver necklace on the beaches of Tijuana are the same people who take a bath when it comes to buying a car back home. The difference is at home they don't realize they are in a negotiation. They don't realize that everything is a negotiation.*

Negotiating is cultural and universal, and it's happening all around us. It has borders. The rules change as we cross those borders, so unless we are aware of them, we'll run into trouble. For the most part, we need to think outside of our North American trust box of complacency and realize that even when we think we're getting a good deal off the start, it could be better. Accept nothing as it is.

Question everything through the eyes of a negotiator.

I learned this by travelling the world. Head to a high-end art dealer in Shanghai and make an offer on a world-class painting; it's as negotiable a purchase as everything else in Asia. Try to buy flip-flops or tequila in Mexico and you will be engaged in a similar experience where the seller starts with a number much higher than they anticipate they will get and your ability

---

* For more on this check out Riding the Waves of Culture by Franz Trompenaars.

to negotiate dictates how much of a winner they become.

Early in my career when I went to China, I learned the culture, table manners and how to hold my sips of 90-proof Baijiu during meetings but, most importantly, I learned how to negotiate. In fact, it was the very first thing our language teacher taught us. Rather than polite greetings or how to say which country we were from, she taught us how to negotiate.

Make no mistake, whenever someone is selling, no matter what they are selling, they will never be as committed to the price as they will be to the sale. They can always settle for less, you just need to know how the transaction works.

Whether on the beach or in the office, sellers will size you up by the clothes you're wearing, your opening line, your posture, your sweaty palms and your overall ability to speak their language, be it Spanish or industry-specific jargon. The rest of the negotiation is basically a game.

Just like any other skill, practice makes perfect when it comes to negotiating. The Chinese language classes almost killed me. Luckily, while I'm a very slow learner, I supplement that by being even slower to forget. In fact, there are three phrases in Mandarin I can still say with the correct inflection:

"How much?"

"Too expensive."

"Can it be cheaper?"

No matter the language, those three phrases should be asked in just about every major purchasing decision.

In my experience—and as anyone who has ever sold to a good Chinese negotiator in business or at a garage sale can confirm—they are persistent and passionate about getting a better deal. In contrast, it's common for emotion to overtake the North American perception of professionalism in an attempt to get what they want.

I've witnessed this show of emotion, voices raised and arms flailing, on both sides of the ocean, but what I found particularly fascinating and exciting in China was that what could be viewed as a brutal, calculator-shattering, yelling match of a negotiation, would often end with a high-five or a handshake when the deal was done. Just like two NHL teams cordially shaking hands at centre ice after a hard-fought playoff series, so too were these business people able to separate themselves from the emotion of the negotiations, knowing they had given it their all and left nothing untried or unsaid.

Quite often in China I would receive a pat on the back or even a hug from my counterpart after a negotiation. Then they asked where I was from. When I said Canada they often high-fived me and said Canadians are good negotiators. But they high-fived everyone.

That's a pretty good outcome for an interaction when you know everyone is stretching their version of the truth. But knowing there's subterfuge is key. In China, I'd go to a market and buy nice fake watches for $5 each. CEOs of big companies where negotiation was key to their business would buy the same watches for $100. People often get taken advantage of when they don't read between the lines and understand that the beginning of every transaction is the entry to a negotiation.

There are many different possible outcomes to every transaction you begin. Even winning isn't cut and dried when you consider the fact so many people walk away from a purchase oblivious to their overpayment. That's capitalism at its best. That's why for me to be satisfied in a negotiation, simply "winning" is not enough. I want to make sure the side that settled for less feels like they got what they wanted. Game. Set. Match.

At its root, negotiating is about understanding and studying human nature and culture.

To do it well, you must know how to look somebody in the eye to see whether they have the same conviction to their cause as you. You must be able to hear the slight quiver in their voice when they aren't sure. You must notice when someone's words and body language don't add up. It comes down to asking your opponent the right questions to understand the value they're actually out to get.

The art of negotiation is about more than clever words. It's about learning everything you can about the other side, both leading up to the negotiation and during the negotiation itself.

PRACTICING THE EVERYDAY NEGOTIATION

Earlier I mentioned negotiations happen every day, all around us, regardless of whether or not we are aware of it happening. This means learning the skills of negotiation can also happen anywhere, at any point in a future salesperson's life.

Some of us learned this skill growing up. Others received a traditional education or were immersed later in life in a culture where negotiation is an aspect of daily life.

Regardless of where you're at currently, or how you have been trained in the past, I think the best way to learn what works in negotiations is to practice.

To start, stop accepting the price you're initially offered and see if you can't get anyone, at any time, to engage in practice negotiations. You'll quickly experience the rush that comes with going into battle every day and appreciate the thrill that comes when you know you negotiated a price down as low as possible.

Or, you'll quickly realize that you're not cut out for this type of thing and should instead trust the negotiations, especially for major purchases like your next home, to someone who is an expert. It's why experts in this area are well paid and in high demand.

For the most part, rules are made to ensure things run smoothly. Early in life we learn the referees and teachers of the world all enforce rules that make the world a more fair, safe and respectful place to be.

But how does blindly obeying the rules and staying well within them help a person get ahead? Because last time I checked, our world rewards those who know how to work within and challenge the system much more than those who simply obey it.

Let me put it another way. Who understands more about why not to touch a hot stove? Is it the child who disobeyed his mother and touched it anyway, or is it the child who obeyed all the rules without question? Experience on both sides of every situation is what develops true savvy. While someone who understands the rules may make for an excellent student or child, it's not necessarily the person you want representing you when a sale that affects the rest of your life is at stake.

When it comes down to negotiating, completing and agreeing to a deal, you want someone who operates on the right side of the tracks, but who understands the world on the other side. It comes right back to understanding the system in place, why it's in place and what needs to be done to successfully work within it.

There is no better example of this in the world than an amazing defense attorney I've had the pleasure of knowing and working with. No, he didn't defend me, but I've been in the courtroom while he worked his magic.

For the first part of his very successful career he was an undercover RCMP officer, investigating and busting members of some of the most notorious drug-trafficking gangs in the country.

Fast forward. Today he's undoubtedly one of the most successful and highly paid defense attorneys around. He understands the system, its rules, where the line is and knows how to keep his clients on the side they want to be on.

It's thanks to my ability to understand, work and even bend the rules of the system that makes me successful today.

I know how to hustle and what being hustled looks like.

I know how to leverage the great people around me and add exceptional value to their situation when needed. I know the importance of having amazing connections in life.

Each and every person I'm connected to I value immensely. I know how and where to ask for help when needed. I can get the people around me to offer a hand up rather than a handout. It's one of the most valuable things I can do.

I can read the signs and ask the right questions to determine what people need to hear, what they want to see and what they inevitably want, regardless of whether they know it or are able to communicate it clearly in the moment. I especially know how to do it when the pressure is on. Plus, I really love to negotiate.

CHAPTER 3

Positively Dennis

"Ah, but a man's reach should exceed his grasp,
Or what's a heaven for?"

—Robert Browning,
poet and playwright

ENTHUSIASM

Iwear my energy on my sleeve. Ninety per cent of the time, that energy is enthusiasm and to me, enthusiasm is what makes the world go 'round. My energy makes everything from my marriage to my company run better. On the off-chance my energy is bad, I don't try to hide it. In some cases, I'll leave the office so I don't affect the momentum of the rest of the team.

In other cases, like when the market is stuck in a downturn and it's making it hard to feel like my typical enthusiastic self, I'll address it with my team. They're probably feeling the drain on their energy too. If something isn't working, we need to acknowledge it and figure out a plan to fix it.

The majority of the time, though, I bring the enthusiasm. And that's what sells. Enthusiasm has been my flavour of the day for most of my days. I got this from my mom and her outlook on life. Every time I see her, she's wearing a smile and bringing a massively positive attitude. She's one of the few people in this world who truly believes that the sun will always come up tomorrow. Even when times were tough growing up, if there were days where the sun didn't seem to be coming up, she made sure we could go out and find it.

I had to learn this from my mom. It wasn't just genetic. Growing up with very little meant every bit of goodness was a massive deposit into my bucket of appreciation. I still feel that way today.

My own enthusiasm and positive attitude has led to the bulk of my success in business and in day-to-day results with clients. When I am with a client, an attitude of appreciation makes it easy to go the extra mile for them—especially when they share my sunny outlook.

Buyers, clients and other people I see appreciate my high energy from the first "Hey!" on the phone to the high-five I get after the lawyer finalizes their deal.

There's just something about nice, passionate people that makes me want to work just a little bit harder for them.

Mom is a big part of why I'm so enthusiastic, but way before I could learn that lesson from her, I survived a very difficult situation. I was born three months premature with a hole in my heart. Doctors said I had a 5% chance of living.

A little perspective. A 5% chance to live meant that if my

survival was a game of poker, I would need to get the one card I needed when the dealer flipped the turn. Or, if we were throwing two dice, and I needed to roll a one and a two on my first roll, my odds on that roll would be better than my odds to live.

On the bright side, my chances of living were better than the odds of rolling a Yahtzee in one roll. But still. No betting man would take those odds.

The hospital staff were so convinced I wouldn't make it through the first night, they called the family minister to baptize me and told my parents to make arrangements for my passing.

I can only imagine how heartbreaking it must have been for my young parents to hear I was unlikely to live through the night. It wasn't until the birth of my own son some 36 years later that I recognized a fraction of the true impact of my parents' emotions.

Through some miracle, I survived the night, and the first week and the first year. I had pneumonia a few times during that first year, had to be fed through a straw and sported a concave chest that stuck with me until I was six years old.*

Did I mention I was obsessed with the next breath of accomplishment? At times that literally meant my next breath.

The complications I experienced as a child helped me appreciate the life I've created and the simple fact I have been given

---

* The chest thing was kind of cool because at the local pool or during bath time I could play with my little toy cars and G.I. Joe action figures using the hole in my chest as a feature in a homemade obstacle course. The kids at my school loved it and it made show-and-tell very interesting.

life. I don't think you necessarily need to have a near-death experience to appreciate life, but it certainly has an impact.

It's the kind of thing that will make you believe that anything is possible. It sounds like a cliché until you've lived it. Time really is precious.

I embrace health in all areas, whether relationships, exercise, diet or attitude. Being positive and enthusiastic not only sets me up for success in my personal life, it helps me in business as well.

MY ROUTINE

I've learned what makes me tick and getting to know myself was essential for me to develop a routine. Routines make or break us as successful adults. They set us up for success or failure.

Making a routine isn't rocket science, but there is some science to it. Experimenting is the key. Once you find what works for you, do more of it. When something you're doing isn't yielding positive results, get rid of it.

For me, part of the formula of my routine is accepting that I'm addicted to approval. This is what drives me through my daily routine. At one point in my life this need for approval led me to be the class clown. Today, it's led me into an industry that rewards me in all of the right ways to feed my pursuit of becoming a world-class real estate salesperson.

One of my goals in writing this book is to help others learn what drives them and how to use that to find their better by sharing my own journey. Figure out what drives you, go after it and leave the rest behind.

I know my strengths and my weaknesses and the stimulants that act as a catalyst for either category. I've learned I'm most successful when I stick to a routine that maximizes my strengths. This means being in charge of the food I eat, what I allow into my head, who I see and what I do.

It's all my way of being positively the best man I can be.

My best friend and one of my mentors, Cary Mullen, is a two-time Olympian and a World Cup champion. He set a long-standing world downhill speed record in Kitzbuhel, Austria when he skied 97 m.p.h. in 1997. He did it by following what he calls his "profitable routine."

Here's my own profitable routine.

5 a.m.

One of the most important commitments I make each day is the time I'm going to get up the next day. I set this the night before and stick to it. Keeping this commitment helps keep me on track throughout the day. Getting an early start also allows me time to work through anything that could negatively affect the day.

When my iPhone alarm goes off, I see the message on the screen, which has been the same for years. It says, "Committed or interested?" That's a line from Tom Ferry. What it means to me is that in life, we're interested in far more things than we are committed to, yet we can easily spend more time and energy on the mere interests.

Interested means you'll do it if it's easy and convenient. Committed means you'll find a way no matter the obstacles. Television is an interest, my marriage is a commitment. I've heard it explained this way: when you're eating bacon and eggs, the chicken is interested; the pig was committed.

Without exception, at one point or another, those things I am committed to were each weighed against other options and came out as the best possible choice for me to spend time on.

Ask yourself, what are you committed to and what are you interested in?

That which I am committed to, I've written down and verbalized. I've set up ways to remain accountable for each one.

5:45 a.m.

I make sure the first thing I put into my body is something that contributes to my energy and health. They say breakfast is the most important meal of the day, and yet how often do people settle for a sugary coffee and a carb-loaded bagel and cream cheese as their go-to?

For me it's all about my green shake. I pack as much nutrition into my morning shake as possible: kale, spinach, half a green apple, half an avocado, half a banana, frozen mango, coconut water, a teaspoon of maple syrup, two scoops of protein powder and some omega-3 oil. I'll have half the shake for breakfast and the other half after my workout, along with a Clif bar or some oatmeal to round out the meal. Also, I prep most of the shake (minus the liquids) in the evening so my work in the morning is minimal.

The shake is breakfast six days out of the week. On the seventh day, I'll add something like half a grapefruit, a handful of almonds and some eggs.

Starting the day healthfully keeps the rest of the day feeling healthy. Plus, not having to think about what to have for breakfast saves my energy for other things.

6:30 a.m.

Leave for the office. I like to get into the office early in the morning. We have ongoing construction outside our office that begins around 7 a.m., and my goal is to be in my desk working before they start.

6:45 a.m.

Arrive at the office.

There's something energizing about the quiet and calm of

the early morning. Those lucky enough to witness it are treated to a world untouched by the stress to come later in the day. For me, it's the perfect moment of serenity my mind needs to get the best start possible.

I turn on my desk lamp and pull out my yellow pad. Every morning I write down my "10 and 10." It's 10 things I'm grateful for and 10 things I want to accomplish in the next few years. I'm careful that the 10 things for the future are all phrased as if I've already accomplished them.

7:15 a.m.

Tackle the email beast.

7:30–9 a.m.

Nobody is allowed in the office before 10 a.m. I have worked this into their employment contracts. I don't think anybody minds. One day someone came in early and I was working with my shirt off. I would often take my shirt off to work because it got damn hot in our old office and we couldn't control the heat.

I usually won't take phone calls before 10 a.m. Not even from my wife. If it's urgent she will text. This rule for me started a few years ago when I had a particularly difficult phone call early in the morning that was so emotionally draining that I found myself useless after the conversation. Some people, whether they know it or not, drain the energy you need for your own commitments. For the first three hours of the workday, I put only good things in me.

9 a.m.

Schedule conference calls and otherwise plan and make notes for the day and the week for our team.

10–11:30 a.m.

Gym time. For me, the 90 minutes at the gym in the morning is time spent working out both my body and my mind. Whenever I'm working out I listen to talk radio or audio books. The uninterrupted time where I get new information and new ideas allows me to keep dreaming.

I love energizing my muscles through a workout and my body with nutrition, but my mind is my favourite thing to work out. I've been doing this since my days in the dental lab when I would clip the handheld radio onto my belt and put on a set of headphones. I'd cycle through my top 20 motivational books on tape and occasionally dive into some spirituality that was broadcast on the radio. For me, the easiest way to keep new information coming is to combine learning with other activities.

12 p.m.

Lunch meeting. I do my best to fill up my lunch schedule every day, the week in advance. If I'm not meeting a prospective client, somebody to network with, or a current client, then I'm absolutely going to be meeting a team member to do some brainstorming or a quick check-in.

1:30 p.m.

Business or team meetings. I will either have an off-site meeting with a prospective client or schedule an in-office meeting to cover off one of the areas we are focused on, whether it be new projects, team development or client maintenance. We also have a weekly team meeting to facilitate communication and ensure alignment among the team's objectives.

3–5 p.m.

This is the best time to address clients' offers as it's usually towards the end of their day. Otherwise, I'll head off to listing presentations out of the office or have clients come to our office.

5–6:30 p.m.

This is a great time to do some community-specific marketing through door-knocking, flyer delivery, creating new listing announcements or putting up signage in our targeted communities. Most people are just arriving home and preparing for dinner. In our city, it gets dark early and it's a great time to target homes in specific communities that have lights on. I find this saves time and energy on what is normally a very arduous task. Catching people home when you are door-knocking is essential.

7 p.m.

Home for dinner and family time. This is my most important meeting of the day. Being home for dinner happens almost every day.

9:30 p.m.

Wife and couch time. One of our favourite times of the day is this rare one—the time when my wife and I catch up, tackle family projects and just chill out on the couch.

11 p.m.

Bed time. The real secret for me in all of this is "balance." I think for a lot of people the word "balance" on its own is completely misleading. I think people presume balance is actually possible. Nope. Balance doesn't happen on its own. And it's relative to each person.

Here's what balance means to me.

I go to bed thinking of the things I need to do tomorrow. I ensure there is time set aside in my calendar to achieve maximum results in each of the four areas that are most important to me at this stage in life.

- ○ Family
- ○ Team/business
- ○ Faith
- ○ Fun with friends

If I can hit three out of the four areas with maximum efficiency every day, I believe I am living a "balanced" life.

If I try to go full tilt in all four areas, I feel distracted. But anything less than three makes me feel guilty. These are my priorities and these are the things that, when executed, allow me to feel balanced.

Maximum efficiency means I go into each scheduled meeting with a plan of some sort so there's no wasted time. This is true even in the playtime my son and I have scheduled every night before his bedtime. He and I both know it's coming. It's either bath time or Hop on Pop. He expects it and I have to prepare for it. Some meetings take more preparation than others, but no meeting should ever happen without an agenda. Not even bath time.

CHAPTER 4

It pays to care

"The rule of my life is to make business a pleasure, and pleasure my business."

—Aaron Burr,
vice-president of the United States of America, 1801-05

IT'S NEVER 'JUST BUSINESS,' BECAUSE THAT WOULD BE BORING

Without exception, you show me someone who is successful in sales and I will show you someone who is great at making and maintaining relationships.

Selling is all about understanding that everyone is a potential buyer, but not everyone is a potential seller. In that same vein, eventually everyone buys something, but they won't eventually buy from everyone.

Sales requires right-fit relationships. Relationships are built on trust and trust is earned through effort.

GETTING PERSONAL
WHEN WORD-OF-MOUTH GOES DIGITAL

Sales is personal. This is true more today than ever before. Today, people make their buying decisions based on how they feel about the brand or individual they are purchasing with. And they'll often make those buying decisions based on how their friends and family feel about the brand or person. This is especially true when it comes to commission sales. It's rarely about the product and more often about the salesperson and overall human connection.

Gone are the Mad Men days where a traditional advertising campaign could convince swaths of the population of a product's or idea's merits. Yes, there was a time before Google, before consumers did their own research to figure out whether the claims in a glossy magazine were true.

For better or worse, we've become a society that is wary of advertising. Instead of trusting the billboards, we rely on personal experiences and real human reviews before we trust a product or a salesperson.

It used to be folks could learn about a new product or service over coffee or at church from someone they trusted. It was personal. Today, word-of-mouth happens online. Online communities, forums and review sites are filled with the experience of dozens or hundreds of people.

Today's word-of-mouth advertising matters more than just about every other piece of marketing material combined. And it's still personal. What people used to tell their close friends in the coffee shop, they'll now broadcast to everyone they sort of know on Facebook, and whoever will listen on Twitter.

Here is where we as salespeople and businesses that sell products come in. We need to do our best to harness the power of the positive vibe. Our focus should not be on the fact that customers may say negative things. Rather, we should focus on how we get them to say positive things. How do we get them to engage in positive conversations?

A lot of this is done unconsciously by our clients online. Someone who posts a picture of their awesome brunch, their new car or their first house to share their joy isn't necessarily intending to tell their friends what to buy. But whether they realize it or not, they're triggering a thought in everyone who sees that social media post. "Oh, I haven't eaten there yet." And that authentic moment of celebration is one of the best word-of-mouth marketing moments you could ask for.

Now, when it comes to online reviews, emotions largely drive what people post. It's been generally understood that at least twice as many people will share a negative experience as will share a positive one. Ouch. It doesn't take long before those told about this crummy exchange of goods and services tell others.

With today's online conversations, the reach for negative reviews is even more than it used to be. A negative message can get beyond your control, accelerated by social media and online sharing tools to reach thousands or even millions of people.

People don't just rate their experience at a restaurant by how much they tip. And people complain because it's easy to do.

If there are issues we can't fix, at least we can always learn from failures. I always call clients who choose to take their business elsewhere. I've got to know why. Feedback unspoken is a killer in the long run.

There's a bright side. I'm seeing a shift happening on social media. It's no longer so acceptable to use it as a platform to complain (especially just for the sake of complaining). I'm seeing social media used as social bragging; about success, a great experience, a perfect meal or a killer workout. Do your best to be something that people want to brag about.

However, if negative comments come your way—and they will—the first step to dealing with it is knowing it exists. When we're aware of where the complaint is coming from, we can deal with the issue head-on. I'm always impressed at how a situation gone wrong can be turned around when my team jumps in to deal with it from a caring place. In the online world, being seen trying to fix a problem gets us on the good side of a community.

In that same vein, if online reviews are coming from people who get a kick out of maliciously complaining, the rest of a community can figure that out too.

With all that in mind, the most important aspect of everything we do as salespeople and marketers is aimed at one objective: start and maintain conversations. Here's how you can get those conversations happening on your own terms:

- Ensure you are encouraging and seeking out new reviews from your clients.

- Have an amazing online presence, including your website, blog and social channels, that invites and allows conversations while feeding your brand and being informative and easy to use.

- Give people reasons to say great things about you.

Word of mouth is not small-time advertising anymore—it's bigger than huge. Regardless of what you spend or who you hire to market your brand, it will never be enough to counter a message broadcast by someone who had a bad experience. No matter how many Google AdWords you buy, nothing will ever pay you as well as a positive comment or review.

WHAT TO DO WITH NEGATIVE FEEDBACK

Nobody is immune to criticism. If you're not messing up somewhere, you're not trying hard enough. Even with the very strictest adherence to the highest codes of conduct, we can't eliminate negative chatter. At some point in time, someone will post negatively online about you for the world to see. Don't let this discourage you. One of the most effective ways to establish yourself as caring and trustworthy is to effectively manage negative feedback.

My team solicits feedback at every opportunity with surveys and follow-up calls. Hearing about the bad ensures we can make the best even better.

You've got three opportunities when you find yourself dealing with a disgruntled customer. You can:

1. examine the cause of the experience.
2. ensure you take responsibility for any fault that is yours.
3. respond in a way that supports your service claims.

If handled professionally, your response to negative feedback can in and of itself create positive word-of-mouth. You've given the public proof that you'll do what it takes to ensure customer satisfaction.

The golden rule on our team when responding to feedback is made up of three simple parts. (It never matters who is right or wrong.)

1. "You're right."
2. "I think I understand. Please tell me more."
3. "Let me see what I can do about it."

Dead simple, right? This will almost always defuse the situation, make them feel heard and appreciated, and open it up for further discussion.

BUILD OR BREAK YOUR REPUTATION

Each interaction your brand has with customers, be it at your office, viewing your ad or attending an event you sponsor, represents a chance to build or break your reputation and, in turn, establish what people say to their friends (and their Twitter followers).

Building your reputation doesn't end with the first impression. Although I firmly believe we need to focus more on prospecting rather than celebrating our last sale, we also need to take time to say thanks. And, if necessary, we must learn where we most impressed or where we failed to meet or exceed expectations.

Many good businesses operate with blinders on. They're like race horses shooting off in pursuit of the next milestone. But one misstep and even a thoroughbred is at risk of catastrophic failure. We've all got to take time to hit the brakes and look around. That means saying, "thank you," and then, "Where could we have done better?"

Irrelevance happens when we're not looking, we don't care or we think we're too good. Find the negative in every single sale. Always, always, always stay in touch with past clients. Say "thank you" as often as possible.

WHY BOTHER WITH AN UPSET CUSTOMER

Your last sale matters more than your next one. First, there's the simple fact that it costs 10 times as much to attain a new client than retain an old one. That means if you fail to correct a hurt relationship, you're basically using wads of cash as kindling to burn the bridge. Second, if I nurture and care about the last client immensely I won't have to worry as much about getting the next one. I'm not saying you shouldn't put forth the same effort, I'm just saying you don't have to struggle as much. About 85% of all our business every year is repeat and referral. This is a direct result of happy clients.

Showing that you care enough to address a client's concerns may be enough to quash any negative feedback, but even better returns will come if you use the opportunity to go above and beyond. You can ensure you maximize a client's experience— and, if necessary, salvage it—by going above and beyond what they expect. The more you go above the call of duty, the better the chance that your efforts will become positive word of mouth.

GIVE YOUR CUSTOMER A DEAL

In my experience there's no better way to maximize a customer's experience than allowing them to feel like they got a deal.

It's become cliché that people respond well to the idea they're getting more for less, but only if they "act fast." Yeah, it helped sell vacuums that cut hair, but it's also the reason you have clothes in your closet you've never worn. Humans have a tough time saying no to a perceived deal. In fact, it doesn't even have to be a deal. It just has to feel like a deal and we can't help being tempted.

There are a few ways to structure your offer so that a prospective customer perceives it as a great deal. It starts with knowing what the customer wants. When you're lucky, what they want is something straightforward, like a particular price. More often, what they really want from their salesperson is a mix of things:

- support
- an unexpected gift
- understanding their need to be listened to
- follow up
- signs of empathy and commitment

Being creative beyond your title is key here.

How do you find out what a customer wants? Each person is different. You'll have to ask questions and which questions you ask will be unique to what you're offering.

Your goal is to understand a person's story and his or her needs, likes and dislikes. Develop questions to elicit emotion and real responses. Create scripts if you need them. You want to know what they need most, what they need least and what exactly are they looking for beyond price. Find out what would be their cherry on top of a great deal.

Once you have information about what they need, you can position the experience of the sale as something special for them. It will help them achieve a goal, and you can give them something extra and unexpected, but highly valued. Once that special something has been positioned as something achievable only by your hand (via your abilities, team, diligence or connections), you can turn a prospective customer into a loyal client.

CASE STUDY:
HOW I FIGURE OUT THE UNEXPECTED GIFT

When I first started in the real estate business, I did my best to say "Thank you for trusting me with the biggest transaction of your life," in a very special way to every client who bought or sold with me. I made sure to customize both the gift and the means of delivery for each.

There is a reason we have two ears and one mouth. Cookie-cutter gifts just have to stop.

Through the years, I've sent baby baskets and Dyson vacuums, cookies, bottles of wine and scotch, gift cards for dinner at their favourite restaurant, and books we've discussed or that reflect what I've learned about their passions. I've found bar fridges for bachelors and stocked them with beer before possession. I've assembled custom coffee table photo books for clients who had an extensive history or sentimental attachment to properties they sold with me.

One of my favourite things to do for a client is purchase the particular items that get negotiated out of the main deal. Sometimes the seemingly small things that really matter to clients get overlooked during the negotiation. For example, one client reluctantly agreed to include a beloved chess set in the sale of their home. I negotiated a side deal after the sale to exclude it. Another time, I negotiated for some patio furniture that my buyer coveted, but which the seller wouldn't initially give with the sale.

All it takes is the look on the client's face when they see the patio furniture on possession day or unwrap the chess set to know it was the right gift.

Giving gifts was simpler early on because I had fewer clients, but it remains at the top of our priority list and it's one of the things I get most excited about.

About a decade ago I received an interesting page. If you were born after 1990, you may not know a page was a message sent to a little electronic device you'd wear on your belt. Kind of like a one-way text message or a message in a bottle. The page was a request for information on one of my listings in a distant part of a suburban community. The page read something like:

"Please call me with price and address. Does it have a view? I need a wood-burning fireplace. Want to see ASAP."

My first thought was it had to be one of my friends playing a lame prank on me. I didn't really have any clients back then, but I was new in the business and I needed a sale almost as much as I needed a full night's sleep.

I arranged to meet this mysterious guy outside the suburban property 15 minutes later. He was driving a used, under-sized pickup truck that bottomed out when he pulled into the parking lot. After only a few minutes of viewing the property he made it clear that this was not the property for him, but he was still interested in seeing what I could offer him. He told me he had a few specifics in mind:

1. The property had to have a great view.
2. Underground parking was a must.
3. It absolutely needed a wood-burning fireplace.

At face value, it doesn't sound like such a tough request. But in this city at the time it was a feat to find a high-rise property with both a view and a wood-burning fireplace. I took my fine-toothed comb back to the office though and within a couple weeks found him what he wanted. It was a sub-penthouse with a view and the fireplace.

He paid cash and we had a deal. Over a celebratory dinner that night he explained to me exactly why he had been looking for such a specific property. He'd spent the better part of his life in the Yukon. He and his wife had joked for years that one day they would settle down into something more urban where they could still enjoy a view.

There was one issue with their new home. Who would bring the wood up the elevator? For years they had fought about who would go in and out of the property when it was −50 degrees Celsius to get more wood to keep their Yukon home warm.

Boom.

That was it.

Fast-forward to possession day. I knew the perfect gift for him would be a full cord of fresh-cut wood for he and his wife to enjoy in their new fireplace. I tracked down a local supplier thanks to a sign on a telephone pole and hired a few kids to help me haul it up the elevator (in 10 trips).

Everything seemed perfect. He was overjoyed with my creativity and attention to the details he had shared of his life.

A few weeks after his possession I phoned him to see how the new condo was doing. (By the way, how many clients have you called back after the sale? I find very, very few people in sales follow up with a prospect in any way.) Everything was great, he told me. He didn't mention the firewood, so I had to ask, "How's that awesome firewood?"

Silence.

He reluctantly told me that unfortunately the wood I had gotten him was a little wet. By "a little wet," he meant it would take at least a year for it to dry out. Man, was I crushed. Doubly so because not only had I secured him a full cord of wood, I had also gotten myself a good stack of logs from the same guy and stored it in our garage. Lo and behold, when I tried to burn one, it did nothing but smoulder. It would sit unused in our garage for a long time.

Thankfully, my effort to make his possession extra special was not overlooked. The personalization of such a gift was the point. He was very happy overall and we both eventually had wood to burn and stories to tell. Find ways to be memorable after the sale.

On my team, we send thank-you gifts for clients, and also to the people who connected us. We often send a thank-you gift just for the act of the introduction, regardless of whether we end up closing a deal.

We send a lot of gifts and so should you.

I mean a lot.

I was audited early in my career. The government only had one issue with my returns; the amount of "client gifts" we purchased and claimed as necessary business expenses. After a thorough explanation, they bought into the fact that the majority of our business is based on the relationships fostered by how we express our gratitude.

WHAT ABOUT WHEN THINGS GO WRONG?

Something went wrong? Great. This is where serious referral business can be generated. It gives us an opportunity to really shine. And if we can't shine, then we can ensure we make changes so we can be in it for the marathon.

It's essential to create a plan for when things go wrong and that requires having reliable contacts who can fix problems. Any misstep that has happened more than twice on our team is a problem we have a plan for. Remember: if you haven't investigated a past problem there's no way you can avoid the next one.

It's easy to celebrate when things are going well. The real cream rises to the top during the hard times. Our team is relentless in our pursuit of making things right. Especially when things go wrong, it's essential to make sure the new result is better than good and the customers better than satisfied.

For example, there is no guarantee a property will be clean for a client to move into on possession day. Unfortunately, it's not contractual. It's assumed that the property will be in the same condition as when the purchase agreement was reached. However, as that's not always the case, we always have cleaners on standby. If there's any doubt surrounding our client's complete satisfaction, we'll book and pay for a thorough cleaning of the property at our expense, regardless of whose responsibility it was to have the place immaculate.

Similarly, missing or misplaced furniture items that were supposed to be included are immediately replaced at our initial expense. Later, far from the client, the responsibility of taking it up with the appropriate people for reimbursement happens. Don't let small details and big egos get in the way of the pursuit of a happy client.

We have a garage full of used appliances and furniture items that sellers have left behind. Even when it's not our responsibility, and other agents or their clients were neglectful, we jump all over it to make the situation right. You will never look bad when you do the right thing. Especially when it's not your responsibility.

We have a strong list of great connections and tradespeople, from exterminators to roofers, carpet cleaners to plumbers. We have a full-time client service manager to ensure that any and all customer concerns are dealt with as fast as possible.

You may be thinking that this type of thing happens all the time, and it does. But the difference is that we commit to taking control of a situation rather than spending energy pointing fingers. Don't let your client or customer get caught up in whose fault it is.

Rarely will we wait for the other side to agree or take responsibility for the issue. It says a whole lot more to our client when we are ready with an immediate solution. This will always pay us back more in the future than waiting and getting somebody else to take responsibility. That can happen later and it's not something we make the client suffer through.

I'm shocked when I get a call from an upset purchaser's agent, when we have represented the seller, asking us to send over our cleaners to give it a final spit and polish. Step up and step in. Get it done and let's all move on. People love solutions and at the end of the day, clients will usually know who is responsible for both the problem and the solution. They won't forget the person who solved the problem.

Guess which one leads to referrals and repeat business?

EVEN IF IT MIGHT COST $100,000

Sometimes the problem is beyond a simple cleaning or a leaky dishwasher.

The solution to that problem depends on how big a game you want to play. How long are you in this race for? Are you in it for the marathon or the 100-metre sprint? The size of your paycheque will correlate.

A few years ago I was involved with a purchase for a very dear friend of mine. He was a very influential person in my life. I'd connected him with the best-of-the-best in my sphere at that time. I felt I was his guy, his real estate agent, and I wanted my team to ensure he was taken care of 100%.

One of the referrals I made for him was a mortgage broker. The lender initially came through in spades. Verbally. He promised everything my friend wanted to do in regards to carrying their current property, acquiring a new one and moving forward with the build of their future dream home would not be a problem.

At least that's what he said.

When it came to closing, just before possession, it became clear the mortgage broker had over-promised. He delivered an amount $100,000 shy of what was needed.

My friend's dream home and future was at stake. With nobody to blame and nobody to take full responsibility, our clients were about to lose their deposit.

I knew that they were absolutely good for the money. I knew that it was just a matter of timing. I stepped up and offered almost all of the money I had in my bank account at that time. I gave them a $100,000 interest-free loan. It was secured by a promise they would pay me back.

Some say it was a big risk, and it was. At the time it was the right risk, the right investment. It all worked out in the end.

Whether it's soaking wet firewood or $100,000, the intention is the same: client satisfaction.

RELATIONSHIPS MATTER MOST

Every year, at minimum, we send every single client in our database a handwritten anniversary letter. We like to do something special for every client annually, too. This year, we created customized calendars with special events happening in our city throughout the whole year and wrote a note in each client's calendar on their birthday.

The primary objective is to reach out to anyone we may have lost touch with, ensure our database is accurate, address any concerns that may be outstanding and find out who has sold without us.

In the same way, we send out client surveys and do our very best to solicit feedback when we sense that anything may have failed within our company. We can't fix what we don't know is broken. We can't know it's broken unless we open the lines of communication. Most things can be solved with money. The one thing you can't fix with money is a broken or unhappy person.

Once, a client emailed to tell me that despite having full confidence in our work, there was one thing that gave them pause. I hadn't immediately responded to an email they had sent about proceeding with a plan to purchase. The clients were uncomfortable with the gap in communication and while they said it was "no big deal" in the end, they thought it was worth mentioning. Which made it a big deal.

That one simple email transformed our business. Our number one value as a team is now responsiveness. We have since worked with this couple on two additional sales.

Responsiveness is key to relationships.

HOW TO MAKE YOUR CAREER IN SALES LAST

As I've gotten older I've realized that not everybody is as interested in other people as I am. Building a long career in sales requires building lasting relationships.

The deeper we can get to know somebody, and the more significant the relationship, the longer-lasting and more profitable the prospect will likely be.

I take for granted that I will get to know most of the people I work with quite well.

Specifically, if somebody calls me to be their real estate agent, I am fortunate to earn a tremendous amount of trust and knowledge from them about their circumstances in a relatively short period of time. We'll talk finances, death, divorce, retirement and the planning of babies. All of this substantially affects a person's real estate plans and possibilities.

In the same way, when people work for our company, we make a point of getting to know them. Until recently I assumed that everybody did this.

I would encourage anybody looking to build a career in sales to stay as curious as possible about others.

Our son's middle name is Stirling. He's named after the home inspector I have used for more than a decade. We've been through a lot together that transcends the few hundred home inspections we've done. Major life events, holidays and, when we get the time, just grabbing lunch. We are friends first and then business associates.

Our real estate lawyer is also a godparent. I met one of the editors for this book when I was in college, and another editor through my assistant at a roller derby convention in Las Vegas.

Just about every person who is associated with our business is someone we've bought or sold properties for. Is it the chicken or the egg? If they give, then I get. But it's because we have given first and gotten to know them that we have received business.

One of the greatest compliments I've received is the trust of those who work with us or have worked with us when they need to buy or sell. From my home inspector to my photographer and lawyer, we've done business with all of them. Yes, it's because we're good at what we do, but most importantly it's because we have great relationships with each of them.

GOOD RELATIONSHIPS MAKE IT HARD TO GET FIRED

Most recently I ran into an issue with the drycleaner that we use. It wasn't them, it was me.

My drycleaner used to operate close to the first property my wife and I owned. I didn't even own a suit when we first met. I would walk down the street and drop off my wife's drycleaning and chat with the owners.

As we got to know each other better, I would bring the owners a coffee from the shop next door or chocolate at Christmas. When my wife and I moved out of the area, they asked if we wanted them to pick up and drop off our cleaning. They said they would start the service just for us. It wasn't because we had a big bill each month, but rather because we had established a great relationship. It was exceptionally kind of them.

Later, they decided to get out of the drycleaning business. In their absence my wife and I found a new drycleaner and befriended the owners. Just a few months later we learned that our old drycleaner and friend was getting back into the business.

We were in a quandary. We'd just gotten to know our new drycleaner really well, but we felt loyal to our first drycleaner. I can't describe to you how difficult it was deciding to break up with one of them. We tried our very best to make it a gentle parting with the second drycleaner, whom we'd gotten to know so well in just a few months. Here's part of the emailed response I received from the new drycleaner:

"My stomach dropped when I heard that you were leaving us. I am reaching out to see if I can rectify anything with you and at least let you know that I care. All customers are important, and you Dennis are very important to me. I reached out in email because I never want anyone to feel like they have been put in an uncomfortable position … I appreciate any opportunity to correct my mistakes."

This wasn't a business responding with some kind of form letter. This is an owner who cares. It was heart-breaking to me that they thought they'd done something wrong.

And then the other drycleaner emailed me (I had told them about our situation). Here's part of what they said:

"Your email is the reason we do our business. The love that we receive and the relationships that we make with our customers is the reason we opened up again … . Again we appreciate you and your family so much and the love and gratitude we have for all of you is endless."

I was touched. We are talking about businesses that care about their future success and show it by caring about me as a customer. Exceptionally well done. We're currently using the services of both drycleaners. Not just because they're both exceptional cleaners, but because we have relationships with both of them.

CHAPTER 5

Thankful for everything. Entitled to nothing.

"The courage to want it all and the ability to live with very little."

–Gary Vaynerchuk,
entrepreneur

CONTENT BUT NEVER SATISFIED

The fact that you're reading this book instead of burning it to keep warm means you likely have reason to be incredibly thankful.

There were times when I was a kid that we could barely afford to take the bus. One day when I was nine I needed to count 75 pennies out of our penny jar so I could take a bus downtown to meet my mom after she was done work. I didn't have a passport until I was 22. Now, I've travelled the world. I'm always shocked when I meet those who have so much, because those people are often the least grateful.

The problem with living somewhere as rich and prosperous as North America, is that often people are not grateful for what they have. It's easy to lose perspective. Instead, they look around at other people's successes in envy. Social media only exacerbates this perception that someone (or seemingly "everyone") is doing better than us. Welcome to the world where everyone has more than you.

But do they?

Just look at the number of frowning faces at the gym or people with no expression at all eating lunch on a patio. Business travellers in first class look like some of the grumpiest people on the plane.

It sometimes confuses me, but deep, deep down I really do understand where it comes from. The key to success is growth and the key to growth is to replace envy with a healthy curiosity and a deep obsession to achieve better.

In contrast, acting entitled, no matter where you live, will not only make you look ignorant, it will kill your opportunity to be successful in sales.

When I see someone who has more than I do, or something that I want, I don't get jealous—I get curious. It's one of my biggest strengths, I think.

Like a child, unaffected by pride and oblivious to image, I'm hungry for truths. I was reminded of this when my son was three years old and we were on a beach holiday. He was learning to make a sandcastle. He noticed another young boy nearby had built an empire of sand. My son pulled me down the beach to investigate, with intense curiosity, what tools the other boy had used, how high he had built it and how he had made the water come in certain parts versus others. That's insatiably curious versus jealous or angry.

I don't want what someone else has earned. I want to discover what they've learned.

My goal, always, is to discover any tips they have and see where their scars are. Then I can adapt those tips to produce my own version of their success. Hopefully without the scars. It's not that I think I deserve what they have—that's entitlement—but I know I can leverage their lessons to go after my goals and get better.

It's the difference between a hand up and a handout.

Knowledge is power and I want as much knowledge as I can get. But the pursuit of knowledge means being willing to swallow my pride and ask for help. I find it's better to ask the stupid question than to stay stupid.

There's no such thing as a person you can't learn something from, but asking the right questions is your responsibility and it isn't always easy. Especially when other people are watching. Especially when the people watching are people who have influence over you.

Our best sandcastles are yet to come if we can just ask enough questions.

HOW DO YOU LEARN TO ASK THE RIGHT QUESTIONS?

Lucky for me, I don't struggle much with asking questions because I know I'm not the smartest person in the room. I strive to surround myself with people who complement my shortfalls so I can be the most inquisitive person at the table.

Here's how I approach the questioning process. First, identify the person's specialty and determine what about it you don't understand. Then you can rely on some simple questions.

For example:

- "Tell me more."
- "Can you clarify?"
- "What exactly do you mean?"

Nobody likes their time wasted, but the thing about people who are successful is they usually like to talk about it.

They say curiosity killed the cat, but I disagree. I think it's actually what made him fat. If knowledge is power then curiosity is king and whoever has the most curiosity will win in the end.

Curiosity can become a permanent state of mind that puts you in a position to identify and draw out the very best of those around you.

PERSPECTIVE AND THE
POSITIVE STATE OF MIND

Your attitude and level of gratitude will determine your altitude of success. Written on the wall of my office is the phrase, "Thankful for everything and entitled to nothing." After all, it takes time to notice the messy stuff. The dirt, the rust, the sharp edges and the reality of life are somewhere in between thankfulness and entitlement. How you view the life you presently lead will determine how quickly and successfully you leave it behind.

As business guru and consultant extraordinaire Jim Collins said, it's about "acknowledging the brutal facts." I can't emphasize enough the importance of a positive state of mind. It goes hand-in-hand with acknowledging what areas of yourself need improvement. Regardless of how difficult or fortunate our past has been, acknowledging reality and the world around us is key. In other words, take time to smell the roses but also take time to notice the messy stuff.

I learned one of my most stark lessons in acknowledging reality while on a remote stretch of a Mexican highway. I was traveling into town with a group of friends for dinner and dancing. We came upon a serious accident, which had clearly just happened. There were onlookers all over the place. We saw damaged vehicles and injured bodies.

A good friend and mentor of mine, who had been giving

the driver directions, asked him to slow down so we could take a thorough look at the scene. This received mixed reviews from the people in the van; some were covering their eyes. A few were in tears. It was quite a scene both inside and outside the vehicle.

My friend insisted we slow down and he stared intently out the window, taking in everything about the gruesome scene. We could see the situation was being handled by the authorities—police, medics and clean-up crews were everywhere—yet he took it all in as if it were his job to do so.

Later that evening I asked him why he was so interested in such an upsetting scene. He shared with me his theory of the importance of slowing down and noticing when disaster is close by. Life isn't only about the highs filled with laughter and celebration, he said. It's about contrast. Whenever life seems to offer uncertainty, misfortune, pain and sorrow, taking inventory of those feelings trains us to appreciate brighter days all the more, he said.

Recognize the dark moments, be present, but do not dwell. Always, always, always pursue a brighter day.

THE IMPORTANCE OF HAVING A #$@% FILTER

Even though I almost always have an opinion, I don't always share it. In sales, as in life, there's great value in understanding when to shut up.

I've trained myself to appreciate that I don't always need to be right and I don't always need to be heard. This knowledge didn't come without pain.

Few things in life hurt like the perception of not being heard. It can be frustrating to feel that others, especially those we care about, don't truly understand our situations, emotions or dreams. Truly being heard doesn't require somebody having the answers or giving us anything in return, it simply means we feel they understood us. Yet true understanding happens very rarely.

I've always wished social services had taken the time to talk to me and Daren before they ripped us from our mom.

In the same way, I believe salespeople need to be very cautious in our approaches and diagnoses. It's not a one-size-fits-all world, especially when selling.

My filter has served me well. There have been moments when I thought people needed to hear what I thought, how angry I was, how stupid their actions were and to have the right way to live explained to them in excruciating detail.

That kind of onslaught rarely produces the outcome I want. The fact is, some people simply choose to always be "right," even if only in their own mind. Logic and reasoning have no place there.

Recognizing who those people are and when it's futile to enter into battle with them is an invaluable skill. Taking the time to filter your reaction will serve you well. Then, ask good questions, take good notes and strategize accordingly.

LISTEN TO WHAT KIND OF SANDWICH THEY WANT

As a kid I wished more than anything else somebody would take enough time to get to know all we were dealing with. Enough time to properly diagnose and then recommend solutions if possible. However, it was my experience that people prefer to "fix" a situation. They would offer advice and usually punishment for behaviours that were often the result of misdirected energy, desperation, fear and a perceived lack of options.

It's painful to not be understood. It hurts to not be heard. My son, as a toddler, could only use a few words to express himself. Some of his biggest meltdowns in life happened simply because he couldn't communicate in a way that I understood.

But something magical happened when I laid on the ground and looked him in the eye. When I took enough time to follow his process, allowed him to take my hand and show me where he wanted to go or what snack he wanted from the fridge, we connected. My wife and I had a major breakthrough in our parenting of our toddler. We observed through some friends of ours the powerful parenting tool of giving options. Giving our son options means instead of saying, "We're going now," we simply ask, "Would you like to go now or in two minutes?" He usually defaults for the two-minute option, but the co-operation rate substantially improved when we started showing him we were listening.

When we take the time to understand and listen to each other as human beings, magic happens.

When we make options for our child, we make sure they're clear, not overwhelming in their diversity. The options must move us in the direction we want to go. Communication in sales is no different than it is in parenting. Being able to listen, understand and diagnose a prospect's situation is integral to making a deal happen. We don't live in a one-size-fits-all world, we live in a Subway world. A place where we can go in and create whatever option we want for whatever type of sandwich we want. Extra, extra crispy bacon please!

Listening to customers is the name of the game. Customizing the experience around them is the flavour of the day.

Most importantly: Get to know your prospect and whether, or how, your product is a fit for their unique needs. Diagnose whether their personality is a fit for your corporate personality. Find out if the people and systems you have in place cater to the individual. Will they work well together or will they fight against each other?

I'm all about the soft sell. By "soft" I mean getting to know the prospect and developing a connection with the prospect. If that means connecting on an emotional level over bologna sandwiches and homemade wine without completing paperwork, that's fine with me.

While this kind of connection is not always possible, when it is, it will always produce better, more scalable results.

CASE STUDY:
BE A THOUGHTFUL LISTENER

A client called me once wanting us to market and sell her multimillion-dollar property. She was a referral whom I hadn't met personally. She was no longer living in Canada, but in the beautiful state of Colorado. The first 20 minutes of the call was her explaining to me how magnificent the property back in Canada was. I barely spoke, just listened.

Despite being late for my next appointment, I stayed on the line because I could tell she wanted to talk. She really needed to talk. She indicated the last sales professional she worked with didn't allow this unloading to happen. After hearing about the property, her expectations on price and what advice she expected from her real estate agent, I asked her what was, to me, a very important question: "Why aren't you moving back to Canada?"

Throughout the one-sided conversation, I'd been able to find the pressure point by taking good notes and listening very closely. This one question opened the door to get to know her, her family, her plans and a bit of her story. And, naturally, her deeper reason for selling came out as well. Knowing the reasons behind her sale and that she shared them with me secures our relationship on a loyalty level that I would never betray and I'll likely reap the rewards of it for a lifetime. It was one of the biggest sales for our team that year.

It comes down to being able to listen thoughtfully. We can't really work well together if we don't know each other. And we can't get to know each other without the ability to listen.

In life, there are people who don't listen to the words being said around them. There may be head nods, smiles and supposed acknowledgement of words being said, but they're just waiting for their turn to talk. The reality is some people are talkers and some are listeners.

Great salespeople need to be better listeners than talkers. The finest listeners take notes.

Try it out sometime. For your next sales call, or at your next family discussion with a spouse or child, bring a yellow pad of paper and a favourite pen. I don't think very many people feel fully heard or understood in most important conversations, but by taking notes and highlighting areas of concern and areas that need clarity, you can better identify and address somebody else's situation.

If nothing else, it highlights the importance that you place on the relationship. As a note-taker, you're saying, "I value you and our time together enough to take notes that I'll refer to after our meeting." Go into the meeting prepped with the direction you want it to go, a few talking points that you have written down and be able to be flexible around whatever additional items come up.

16 TIPS FOR GREAT CONVERSATIONS

1. Be prepared. Know your intention for any interaction.

2. Know your audience and what they value.

3. Humans are feelers not doers, so start with a check in. "How are you feeling?" Not, "How are you doing?"

4. Be vulnerable. People tend to match the other person's level of vulnerability and energy. That's how progress is made.

5. Try and feel the conversation. Understand where it's going and why.

6. Identify what is actually troubling the other person. Not what we think it is when we sit down but what it actually is. This requires you to ask questions.

7. Be genuinely curious.

8. Take notes in a way that shows you're engaged.

9. Don't be too quick to offer solutions or advice. Rather, share your experiences and personal stories to relate. Ask if they would like advice and be sure you know what they're actually looking for.

10. Say "Tell me more" often.

11. Don't try to trump them with a "better" or more painful story. Just relate.

12. Thank them "for sharing," not for the meeting.

13. Suggest another get-together for the future.

14. Reflect on the notes you have taken.

15. Send a follow-up email with a few notes to summarize and offer help or resources to any issues you can ASAP. That means the same day whenever possible.

16. Never stop staying in touch until they ask you to.

ONE OF THESE ROADS IS MORE TRAVELLED FOR A GOOD REASON

The road less travelled is not the one for me. Not always.

I get the concept of "the road less travelled," and I think the words combine for some nice poetry, but there is more merit in following the footsteps of those with the courage to go before us; our Sherpas, teachers, mentors, family members and even our competitors. We should follow those who have weathered the storms, have taken the hits and have the scars to show it.

Something very valuable comes from learning from the mistakes of others. Not to say there won't be specific moments and opportunities when we need to take a leap of our own or step past the ones in front of us. Nevertheless, most of the journey can be better experienced, can be more profitable and can better position us for great things at the right time, if we just take the groomed trail long enough.

The road less travelled is a romantic notion. Just compare a start-up to an acquisition; the success rate of a franchise versus a new restaurant; fly fishing a stream with a guide and a boat or just setting off alone with your new gear on a raging river.

Trailblazers are admirable, attractive, mysterious and rare. Successful people who are also great learners of life are more common. The latter have usually chosen the right time to blaze the right trail. And if nothing else, they can pass on any lessons learned when things didn't work out "perfectly."

Don't get me wrong. I'm insatiably curious and I love being an early adopter. I love being the first to try something, I'm OK with making mistakes and I love making people laugh. However, my curiosity is probably what has gotten me into trouble more than anything else. There's a voice inside me that says, "You should at least try. Go ahead! Nobody else has done it and this is your time to shine." But there is also a whisper that asks me, "Has somebody done this before whom you might be able to get some insight from?"

The first voice is not always the voice of wisdom. For example, when I was five and nearly burned down the house after I discovered matches. Or the time, at age 11, when I found some leftover paint in our rental so I attempted home improvements and painted our kitchen cabinets, walls and the burners on the stove. Or the tooth I lost crowd-surfing when I was 15 or the failed personal training business I started when I was 22.

But when the stakes are high for my business or my family, I always lean on expertise before curiosity. I'm all about hearing stories and how others have gotten their scars before I make scars of my own.

REAL R&D IN BUSINESS

I am all about R&D. In most circles, that means research and development, but it's more commonly referred to as "rip off and duplicate" amongst entrepreneurs or anyone who's been to China.

I love coming up with potentially great ideas and being able to run them by a few seasoned and scarred entrepreneurs who have been down a similar path.

Whenever possible I highly recommend vetting your idea with someone who has already done the dirty work.

Talk to the business person who has gone bankrupt doing what you are about to do. Talk to the person who has made millions doing what you are about to do.

Leverage the wins and losses of others around you to fast-track your climb to success.

I don't for a second think making it in business is easy. What is relatively easy, for me anyways, is R&D, or asking for good advice and direction. The world is full of smart people and it's getting easier and easier to access their brains.

I've made a point of knowing when I'm getting good advice and doing my best to not only act on it, but also never forget it.

A few of the most helpful lessons I've learned along the way:

My mom always told me to say "please" and "thank you" more than necessary. She was right.

My mother-in-law's words, "Do your best to give a hand up versus a handout and never refuse the former," have long resonated with me.

My father-in-law told me from early on in our relationship to, "Read everything you can get your hands on and stay in school."

One of my first big-purchase clients, the seasoned businessman Ken Wilson, told me, "If you don't have something nice to say then don't say anything at all. (Especially in a crowd.)"

The minister Billy Graham has famously said, "Avoid how the problem looks and you will likely avoid the problem altogether."

Zig Ziglar said, "Giving is the secret to getting."

From all the best teachers I've learned from through the years, I've developed a few mantras for our team:

- "Treat all people well, but especially your people."
- "Loyalty matters most, and it's a two-way street."
- "Stay in touch with those you love and respect."

So often I see salespeople ask for good advice, but then do nothing with it. They're smacked in the face with opportunity and all they need to do is a bit of hard work and perseverance. But they do nothing.

Actions speak louder than words, for sure, but we need to make sure we hear the wise words that are spoken. If you're lucky enough to hear them, take them to heart and take action on them. You're not just duplicating it because by doing it— whatever "it" is—you will do it in a unique way. As a bonus, you'll have learned from someone else's experience without having to do the work that's already been done.

THE GIFT OF AN OLDER BROTHER

The best source of advice and direction for me early on, bar none, was my brother. Daren paved the hard road for me by going first. That means—invariably—making a few mistakes along the way, as most older siblings do.

I love my brother deeply and he taught me a lot of really important stuff. As young boys, we didn't have role models. That meant he made most of his decisions in a vacuum. He was the first to break a rule, get a spanking, move out of the house, travel, try drinking, hang out with the bad dudes, date the pretty girls. The gamut. Coming after him meant I had the benefit of his experiences to align with or push away from. I can say I was the first one to drive a car, but unfortunately the car I drove was a stolen one.

This is the curse some older siblings need to face. They get to the privileges and consequences first. Our home environment meant it was mostly consequences. His early life was all trial by error and trial by fire.

Fair or not, I had the example of someone else's consequences to learn from. And learn from them, I did. The good, the bad and the ugly. This kept me, fortunately but just barely, on the right side of things in most cases.

I've had to learn from my own mistakes along the way too. Some were unavoidable character-building moments. I thank God for those times and do my best to avoid them whenever possible. They hurt, but they do teach.

Today we can learn from some of the bravest and smartest people in the world with the simple tap of a screen. The "big brother learning academy" is now called the Internet. We can learn to build houses on YouTube and get websites designed for five bucks. Not that you should. But that's what big brothers are for.

Good advice is no longer hard to find. The real difficulty is listening, understanding and executing that advice.

ESTABLISH CREDIBILITY BY BEING TRANSPARENT

When considering someone's advice and direction, it helps both of you to know they're a professional.

I once went on a three-day hiking expedition that involved crampons, tethering and using ladders to walk across crevasses.

I hadn't done any of it before. We were guided by three people, including one person I chose to ignore at a pivotal moment early on in our trek.

As I was attempting to scale a steep incline, tethered by the climber ahead of me who was already up, I reached a spot with a few different options. I looked up to my guide for direction. She pointed out a route that, to me, did not look like the best. And seriously, what did I know? Despite her advice I chose my own route. Bad move. It was an extremely difficult option and only by dumb luck did it turn out to be successful. I wasn't mortally wounded.

I learned later that evening this amazing woman who had given me directions just happened to have reached the summit of Mount Everest. Damn, did I ever feel silly for ignoring her. But to be fair to me, knowing her expertise before starting out on our trek would have been nice. Sharing your credibility and experience matters, and hopefully you can do it before your audience is hanging off the side of a mountain. Metaphorically or otherwise.

Several years ago I was involved in a business group with a collection of high-level business leaders. The facilitator of our group had spent the better part of his career travelling the world and working directly with top executives, business owners and successful entrepreneurs. He often talked about the need to establish credibility from the front of the room right at the beginning of most of his talks. He's right.

When giving feedback or advice, it helps the audience receive it more openly if we establish our credibility by showing our scars and successes. When we're the ones giving advice, we must share real experiences, both the painful and profitable ones.

I have a lot of gratitude for all the leaders out there brave enough to share with us, cry with us and most importantly, bare their vulnerability so that future leaders can stumble less along the way. That's the kind of teaching I love. The alternative is just simply somebody's theories. And I'm not all that interested in theories.

One of the things I enjoyed most about university was the time at the beginning of each semester when professors would take a few minutes to explain the course curriculum, give the highlights of their CV and answer questions before we got started. I loved to ask the profs to share a bit of their previous experience. I wanted details. I wanted to know where they had won, lost and what they'd have done differently if they could do it all over again.

I got a lot of information from this line of questioning. It revealed a tremendous amount about the individual and gave real context for the direction the semester would take. Ultimately, it informed how much I would pay attention in class.

A few of the professors I was most fascinated by became clients shortly after graduation, while others became friends and some of my best referral sources.

CHAPTER 6

The pursuit of better

"The major reason for setting a goal is for what it makes of you to accomplish it. What it makes of you will always be the far greater value than what you get."

—Jim Rohn,
entrepreneur

WHAT GOAL-SETTING
REALLY MEANS

Setting goals is about embracing a state of pursuit. When you pursue goals, you're committing to an unwavering search for something better than what currently exists. Goal-setting means despite how bad or good it is for you in your life, you know better is always possible and you go after it.

"Better" means different things for different people. I still remember passing the second grade, despite having moved schools four times that year and a complete lack of confidence or support offered by my teachers. That success as a seven-year-old, although minor when compared to other struggles I've faced, sticks out in my mind. I realized early I needed to be in charge of my own path because everyone else was distracted with their own. This still stands true for me today. Nobody ultimately cares as much about our futures as we should.

One important goal when I was younger was finishing college. Like my stint in Bible college, I went to business school partly out of curiosity. But I also thought it was what a guy had to do to have credibility in the business world. A couple years into school, I decided I wanted to propose to my girlfriend. I set up what turned out to be a very formal meeting with her parents where I told them my plan. They were silent. Eventually, after we sorted through their many questions, they told me in no uncertain terms that if I was to marry their daughter, I had to complete my college education.

No problem, I thought. I proposed a few days later.

Turns out my future father-in-law was shocked because he thought I had agreed to finish college before any proposal would happen.

So he might have been even happier than I was once I did eventually reach my goal and graduated.

I can't feel the thrill of success on any level until I've accomplished something I've specifically identified as a goal, and have done so in a way that can be measured and considered excellent.

Speaking of which, I was recently nominated for two industry awards. One for "marketing excellence" and another for "community impact." I was totally honoured and the nominations were utterly unexpected. I identify more with being a "finalist" than a "winner." I'm always in pursuit of better. So while I was appreciative of the kind words and recognition, I'd achieved something that I wasn't even aware of. As far as I'm concerned, nothing can be achieved by accident. That is to say, in order to feel a true sense of accomplishment, I need to have been aware of a challenge, set a goal and worked hard to achieve it.

I do feel like I am in pursuit of making our industry the best it can be. In pursuit of leveraging relationships to make our world a better place. In pursuit of creating client experiences that are great, and in pursuit of doing things right and treating people right. As far as I'm concerned, my efforts there are ongoing and nowhere near being fully achieved.

I'm just getting started. I don't need an award, I need a Gatorade.

SET THE RIGHT TYPE OF GOAL FOR YOURSELF

Don't get me wrong, I'm all about recognition. I've built my business culture around the pursuit of goals and the rewards that come with it. But in order to truly feel the sense of accomplishment that comes with achieving a goal, you need to set the right type of goal.

Like everything in life, setting goals is something you need to practice to get good at. When I started setting goals I was paralyzed with the fear of failure. Not because of what failure meant to me, but because I felt others would be disappointed in me.

Thankfully, I eventually realized goals are personal. If constructed and measured using the right metrics, goal-setting can bring a level of satisfaction and fulfilment in life that fully justifies the at-times terrifying risk of failure.

Here's a checklist that works for me in making the pursuit of goals fruitful:

- Does the goal matter to me?
- Is the goal measurable?
- Is the goal centred in reality? (I may love to hike, but I'm not going to climb Everest next weekend.)
- Does the goal impact and reward somebody other than myself?
- Have I written down my goal?
- Have I shared my goal with anyone?
- Am I prepared to put in a ton of work to achieve this goal?

The only way to ensure you stay motivated to achieve your goals is to set them in areas you care about. The Rev. Robert H. Schuller said it well: "If it's going to be, then it's up to me."

I could probably accomplish some goals that belong to other people if I worked hard enough, but even if I did, it wouldn't provide me with the feeling of satisfaction and accomplishment that comes when I accomplish something near to my heart.

Here are some of my goals currently as I write this book:

- Have a second child.

- Be an amazing and connected husband and father every day.
- Build a new house and a new cabin within the next five years.
- Pursue zero personal liability (this does not mean have zero debt; it just means have zero personal liability on our debt).
- Build our team and company to be the most profitable real estate brand in Canada.
- Be connected, as a family, to the most influential people in the world.
- Be one of the biggest givers and donors at our church.
- Start a youth camp to help kids on the edge realize their greatness.

Where you are in your life will drastically affect the way you look at and choose your goals. As a kid, my life was simply about survival:

- Get enough food to eat.
- Make friends.
- Keep Mom safe from anything that might harm her.

I wasn't the type of kid who could afford to consider chasing dreams that required me to accomplish anything beyond the next day. When I was living day-to-day and couch-to-couch, reaching upwards just to touch bottom, the term "goal" seemed meaningless and unrealistic. I had other things to worry about, important things.

What I realize now is it wasn't the idea of goals I was resistant to, it was the idea of chasing someone else's goals. The things I cared about, those were my goals, whether I recognized them as such or not.

Now, my goals have evolved along with my career. My initial goal was simply to make enough money to get out of debt. It was important to me to feel financially secure and not owe anybody—just in case they came knocking.

When I was 16, I'd racked up a lot of debt. The bank called one day to tell me my line of credit needed to have a zero balance every 90 days. I must have missed that when I applied for it. The bank offered no solutions and told me unless I dealt with my debt, they would pursue action.

The feeling of desperation ingrained in me a deep desire to ensure that I could operate financially on my own terms. I've since discovered the driving force behind my professional goals is that desperate feeling. I never want to have that feeling again. I want to protect my family from that feeling too.

Once I accomplished financial stability, I realized there was no guaranteed retirement package in my industry. My new goal became preparing for my future.

Practice setting goals that work for you so you can start pursuing them.

THE MYSTERIOUS MAGIC OF WRITING THINGS DOWN

There's something about the written word that makes an idea real. For me, the act of getting a goal out of my head, written down and out into the world is an important part of my life. Writing it down gives me a chance to edit and sculpt it to perfection. That makes the goal real, identifiable, verified and too legit to ever give up on.

The idea of writing down goals isn't new; it revolves around age-old philosophies on guided meditation, visioning and articulation through writing and repetition.

I had no idea about any of that when I was journaling as a teenager. For me, it was just the best way to express myself when I didn't have anyone to talk to. It was a way to process everything that happened to me.

It's still one of the best tools for reflection and growth that I have. For me, having the perspective of those journals from my youth reminds me of where I came from, how I got here and how much further I can go.

Journaling can simply mean capturing what happened on a given day. I don't have a very good memory, so at its simplest, my journal reminds me what I've been through lately or how I felt when I went through something, and it reminds me why I do what I do. Write down what happened or what is happening and what you feel about it.

Recently I journaled about how distracted I was when I was helping some clients sell their house following a divorce. After I wrote the experience down and thought about it, I mentioned my level of distraction to the person who referred me to the divorcing clients. He reminded me to be at home with my own family. I cancelled some appointments and went straight home that day. Peeking behind the reality of so many people in this business reminds me to appreciate the significance in each day.

But it's easy to forget if I don't write it down.

And when I say write it down, I do mean "write." Despite my atrocious handwriting, I believe writing on paper is a nearly lost art.* The physical act of handwriting something and the time it takes to do so, compared with making a voice note on my phone, or typing it in a document stored somewhere in the cloud is an essential moment of reflection for me.

Seeing my own writing in hindsight is important too. There's a lot of emotion in it. I have vivid memories from childhood of writing down things about where I wanted to go, what I wanted to have, and then most importantly how I was going to achieve or attain it.

These were dreams more than they were goals. In the second

---

* However, I'm glad I didn't obsess too much about learning to spell in school. Technology has mostly taken care of that for us. When the first iPhone came out, it didn't have a spell-checker and I had to hack it so that people could understand me.

grade I wrote that letter I mentioned earlier as part of a class-room exercise. It said: "I get sad when my dad drinks beer and kicks my mom out of the house. I just want to be safe."

Don't miss that this was in Grade 2. I didn't fully realize how jarring the letter must have been for a teacher to read until I was at my son's school, seeing letters sort of like that posted on the wall in the hallways. Except those letters were happy.

When my high school guidance counsellor read my old letter to me in her office, back when I was faced with maybe being kicked out of school for good, it was the first time some-body else became part of my goal: safety.

A more recent goal is the one that I set when starting in the real estate business: obtain one revenue property per year for every year I'm in the business. I wrote that one down when I had a mountain of debt, very little credit and no sales to report. Today my family's rental portfolio has exceeded that goal. Because this goal matters to me, and falls within my area of expertise in real estate, it's something I now pursue with both energy and passion.

Writing is about articulating. It's about clarifying our emotions and dreams, transferring inner energy, pain and ideas into straightforward statements.

They say we don't dream with pictures in mind. Therefore we need to put our dreams on paper so we can focus on making them a reality. Then we can pursue them relentlessly. Writing keeps us accountable to ourselves and our goals.

Some goals are best realized on vision boards.* Vision boards are a way to connect feelings with images cut out of magazines or printed off the Internet. They're a visual collage of goals, ideas and inspiration. I put up my vision board where I can always see it, to remind me of what I am in pursuit of and what I crave.

My vision board is also a way to involve others in my world because it's a visual representation of the swirling ideas and motivations in my head. I like to think the vision board gives people something specific to ask me about and a glimpse of what I'm striving toward. Sharing success and aspiration are equally important.

SAY IT OUT LOUD: AFFIRMATIONS

Affirmations are another opportunity to use repetition to solidify your commitment to your goals. For the longest time, before I tried it for myself, I thought affirmations were for the faint of heart. I've come to realize the importance of repeating a specifically crafted word or phrase targeted at a desired state of being.

Before a meaningful sales call, I'll say a few words over and over again in my car. "I am successful, caring and the best marketer for this project." And repeat. You may laugh at the thought

---

* Erin Skye Kelly does amazing vision board seminars. She's the one who put me onto it and I'd recommend you hire her too.

of a grown man chanting in the car to pump himself up for a sale, but hey, it works for me.

The truth is, we're all very impressionable. The perception people have of us matters. Our skin is rarely as thick as we need it to be. While we'd all like to think the world isn't out to get us, the reality is there are constant attacks on our ability to stay positive and focused on meaningful goals.

To battle back, and help me create the best version of myself, I combat the negative influences on my chi with a lot of positive self-talk. The words, images and feelings I want to experience and be known for are the ones I focus on. At the same time, these affirmations are not just inside my head, and not just spoken, but written down and there for others to see.

Call it fighting fire with fire, call it whatever you need to, but get those goals, those positive representations of the best you imaginable, spoken out loud and down on paper.

KNOCK AND THE DOOR WILL BE OPENED

Getting other people in on your goals can be beneficial for both you and them. In my goal-setting, I start with a list of ideas. From there, I think of people and places I need to visit to make the ideas happen. These are people and places I need to investigate to get closer to making my goals and dreams happen.

Similarly, I believe living large and sharing my goals, dreams and successes with others motivates rather than discourages them. But the sharing has to come from a pure place, not bragging to build up myself over someone else.

People like to connect with each other. Our drive to relate to others is why social media is so successful and why it's relatively easy to get 20,000 people at a sporting event to do the wave.

Share your excitement, your drive and your energy with those around you and you'll soon have your own cheering section. There's always going to be someone who will be resentful of your energy and success, but that should only matter if your goal is to have everyone like you.

Sharing my goals isn't only about accountability for me. The word "accountable" isn't a word that excites me; it seems limiting. On the other hand, "support" is a word I love. Seek out people who will support and add energy to your ideas. People who will rally behind you and offer you the tools and resources necessary to obtain the goals and dreams that you have put on paper. People who will offer you a hand up versus a handout.

If you share your dreams and goals with somebody and all they do is criticize you, get rid of that person.

A MEASURABLE GOAL IS AN ATTAINABLE GOAL

The whole point of making goals isn't to necessarily achieve them but to live in pursuit of them. Make sure your goal has a defined and well-articulated target, but keep your eyes open because the journey is where the real magic can happen.

If we pursue a goal like a hungry dog chasing a hot dog cart, we'll miss what's happening on the peripheries: important conversations, opportunities and other people's feelings, for example. To that end, and by definition, goals need to have a measurable way to gauge success. If a goal isn't done until it's done, you need to know what defines "done."

Keep in mind that some goals take years to achieve and others happen a few moments at a time. It may take years to get out of debt or lose 25 pounds and years more to buy a Tesla. But in a few minutes a day I can meet goals like staying off Facebook for an hour, not losing my temper when "that" happens or driving the speed limit.

Some goals are easy to measure:

○ Obtain 100 rental properties.
○ Earn a million dollars.
○ Graduate college.

Compare those with these more vague goals, which have no clear "done" moment because they are not measurable:

○ Own more property.

- Earn more money.
- Study hard.

I don't recommend writing your goals like the latter ones. It's the measurable goals that make it clear when you're finished. They keep you reaching for something specific and you can gauge progress along the way.

Assuming you start from nothing, owning 50 properties, earning $700,000 and being accepted to college are all signs of progress towards a larger, measurable goal. You can see your progress and you can see a finish line.

Understanding where you sit in relation to the success of a goal can act as motivation to keep going during tough times, seeing what you've accomplished or how close you are to getting there.

All of that said, there will be plenty of magic along the way. Be sure that if you deviate from direct pursuit of your goal, you measure it against the larger target. If the action on the peripheries is getting you too far off track then you may need to do a check swing.

CHASE YOUR UNICORN, BUT DON'T MAKE IT PLAN A

There's a big difference between a wish and a goal. A wish is something that requires divine intervention to accomplish. It isn't something you can work towards. It's owning a unicorn.

It's not real. If you have written down a wish where a goal is supposed to be, it should have a big circle around it and a sticky note that says, "Needs to be measurable and realistic."

A goal, unlike a wish, is something that can be achieved by combining belief with hard work. Hard work is a big part of it. In order to stay motivated, I need to present myself with a reasonable challenge. Something I can fail at, learn from and get back at. Something that hurts a little to accomplish, like a hard hour at the gym or the feeling I get at the top of a mountain.

I'm not saying all goals are tough to accomplish. I'm saying if your goals are too easy, you're selling yourself short of something so much better. Don't give up on the unicorn just to replace it with a hamster.

It's all about starting small and working your way up to what you really want. It's progressive, not settling. I like how Joe De Sena, founder of the Spartan Race, puts it in his book Spartan Up: If you're in a Spartan race, you have to climb over the wall in front of you before you can know what the next obstacle is.

I think sometimes people are most distracted when they think they should be somewhere they're not yet. They try to skip over the steps along the way to bigger goals. That doesn't work and it's a waste of energy.

When I was a teenager with three credit cards, I couldn't even begin to think of preparing for retirement. Later, when I was focused on getting out of debt, it was impossible to imagine having a million dollars in the bank. The big goal was to be debt-free, but that had to be scaled back into small goals: go to work every day, save 10% of everything, cut up the credit cards.

No matter where you are now, you can change direction and with time, sacrifice and hard work, you can accomplish your goals.

Just keep it real. Know where you are and what you can do today, this week and this year to get closer to your goal.

Let's be clear. It's not just about believing in yourself. I might believe that I can slam dunk a basketball, but reality will prove me wrong. I'm only 5 foot 7 and my calves are hardly recognizable when I wear shorts. Despite best efforts, training, preparation and time spent, some things will always remain unachievable to some people.

A big part of keeping your goals challenging but still reasonable is knowing how far away what you want is from where you are today. Being able to recognize exactly where one is in life despite how ugly or dysfunctional it may be, is the first step in moving away from where you are towards where you want to be.

For example, that may mean acknowledging the effect of the economy on your business. For me, it meant acknowledging I'm brutal at spelling and typing and that was going to be a factor when it came to writing a book. Lucky for me, Siri is willing to convert my voice to text, and that's how 90% of this book's rough draft came to be.

As a kid I was self-conscious and embarrassed easily. For a long time I was embarrassed about my reality and allowed that shame to hold me back. It wasn't until I acknowledged the past and learned how to turn that embarrassment into energy that I was able to change my reality instead of using it as a crutch or excuse.

I may not be able to slam dunk, but I'm sure good at stealing bases.

REALITY MEANS REVISING REGULARLY

As I mentioned earlier, I'm deeply obsessed with the next breath of accomplishment. For me it's liberating to be able to earn an income and have security.

I wasn't raised with any false teaching that money and work opportunities fall from the sky. I was fortunate to have a mom and others around me who worked hard and enjoyed being productive. I've been blessed to know that there are good people who are willing to offer a hand up, but that a golden handout does not exist and we must always be willing to get our hands dirty.

I know there's a mountain of psychological and biblical references that speak to the benefits of being content. However, contentment is not a feeling I experience. Thankful, yes. But never satisfied. The more I accomplish, the more I believe even more is possible.

I've always been able to envision where I want to go in life, the things I want to have and how I want to feel. I've always lived a life focused on the future. Some people can get stuck pursuing the same goals, which have either long been accomplished, and present little challenge, or that are so far from being accomplished that a sense of failure has led to surrender.

That's why it's important to revise your goals regularly. I'm not saying to give up on your goals or to renegotiate the goals you've missed. Rather, we need to acknowledge that just as seasons change so too will priorities. Economic realities and world events will ultimately cause us to need to change our focus, as will changes to our family and personal lives.

Be aware and be focused at the same time. Keep yourself challenged. Know where you are in the big picture of your goals and revise before you give up.

Work towards the pony, the horse, the stallion and then, when all else has been accomplished, go find your unicorn.

FAILURE DOESN'T HAVE TO BE PERMANENT

The best part about striving to attain goals is it changes the way we think about failure. Professionals who get paid to speak about success consistently outline the importance of embracing failure as a means of getting closer to success.

Failure is an incomplete sentence. It's a sign you're still

somewhere between your goal and where you started.

Failure only becomes final when you quit.

So hurry up and fail quickly so you can learn from it and be better equipped for next time.

In fact, failure in and of itself can become the goal. It seems weird, I know. But the phrase "No pain, no gain" speaks specifically to failure as a sign of true progress.

Wayne Gretzky said, "You miss 100% of the shots you don't take." The concept is simple and yet so many people I meet believe that staying where they are puts them at less risk of failure than putting themselves out there.

The long list of recognized success stories across all sorts of genres and countries throughout history, from Albert Einstein to Michael Jordan are all, without exception, riddled with failures that predated success.

The difference between the names we remember and the names we have never heard spoken is that true success stories use failures to learn a much-needed lesson and solidify their resolve to press on.

I think it's funny that lessons on the importance of failure are taught today at a cost of thousands of dollars through conferences and self-help books. They're really the same lessons I learned as a seven-year-old. All you need to do to get ahead is learn.

SURROUND YOURSELF WITH GOAL-ORIENTED PEOPLE

Birds of a feather flock together and fail together. And millionaires? Same same.

One of the first things I had to do to put myself on the track to success as a teenager was turning my back on a few of the friends I was hanging around. Anyone stuck in a life or habits they want to change will tell you one of the hardest parts isn't losing the behaviour you are trying to change, it's losing the friendships you have built around having that behaviour in common.

Although my friends back in my early teens were reasonably good guys, we were constantly in trouble. Whenever we hung out it was always just a matter of time before we ended up getting into mischief because that was the only true goal any of us had as a group.

As soon as a better life became a goal for me, I knew I had to make some changes.

Goals become easier to attain when you align yourself with people headed in a similar direction. Just like the trip south becomes more efficient for a flying V of Canada geese, surrounding yourself with others committed to moving in the same direction will provide you inspiration, support and encouragement.

You can't control the impact your relationships have on you. You have some influence, but not enough.

For me, getting off the path to underachieving meant changing schools and developing a new set of friends. I didn't see this, but Mom and the other adults around me did. Sometimes necessary change is placed at your feet and all you need to do is run with it.

It's been said you can change your life by changing your habits. But I say you can change your life simply by changing the people you hang around with. Jim Rohn famously said, "You are the average of the five people you spend the most time with." Ask yourself if that's a good thing or a bad thing for you.

CHAPTER 7

Just say no to always saying yes and do it with grace

"People think focus means saying yes to the thing you've got to focus on. But that's not what it means at all. It means saying no to the hundred other good ideas that there are. You have to pick carefully... Innovation is saying no to 1,000 things."

—Steve Jobs,
co-founder, Apple

BUSINESS IS PERSONAL.
SO IS SAYING NO.

Business is rarely just "business." Anyone who is good at sales can be good at business, but not everyone who is good at business can be good at relationships. For example, when I need to get a deal done, I can simply get the deal done. But I find it more enjoyable and meaningful to build a relationship with the people involved. For me, the joy of sales is beyond making a sale. It's learning as much as possible so my team can go above and beyond wherever possible. This personal approach puts us in a great position to both protect and serve our client.

I'm far more interested in the client who wants to have a real conversation about life than I am the client who just wants to get a deal done. This is my secret sauce and I wouldn't replace it for anything.

You must first say "yes" to get the experience you'll need to be able to say no with grace and confidence. When I started in sales, I said yes to just about everything and everyone. If you are just starting out I recommend you do the same. Say yes, say yes often and stay very, very curious. The time will come one day when you get to say no. It's a luxury to be able to do so.

At first, when I was selling pots and pans, I would host dinner shows and demonstrations for anybody who would give me the time, regardless of their interest level or ability to buy. Then, over the years, as I honed my craft, I became much more discerning of where my time was spent. With practice, I was able to dial into the prospects who had the highest probability of a sale. This came with training, embracing failure along the way and fine-tuning my ability to qualify individuals.

It is about knowing when and how to say no.

When I began my business in residential real estate I hit the pavement hard. I made calls, sent letters, had coffee and let everybody and anybody know I was in the business. I chased new business and old contacts. Any business at all was good business for me. I just needed to be in front of people talking about real estate, learning about real estate, and sourcing any and all leads I could drum up.

If you want a long and prosperous career in sales you can never spend too much time prospecting. Every day and every meeting is prospecting; today's conversations represent tomorrow's business. Prospecting really just means spending time with people, having real conversations face-to-face over a cup of coffee, just for the sake of having a conversation.

At the same time as I was chasing new business, I was exercising my intuitive muscle. I was learning how to identify the characteristics and habits that separated the real buyers and sellers from the talkers.

A lot of my initial business, and to this day the majority of my existing business, has come from friends and family. Many of the friends started as just acquaintances or simply people I sort of knew through a friend. Even going through my high school yearbook and targeting individuals who would remember me was an effective method of prospecting and lead conversion.

However, the friends and family I was closest to were, in the beginning of my career, often the least likely to do business with me. Because they had insight into every little flaw I may have had, they were more comfortable working with someone they didn't know as well. Perception matters more than reality. There are going to be times when friends and family do not make good business partners or clients.

One such situation came via a family member shortly after I got into the real estate business. He knew I was doing fairly well and had gained some experience. He asked if I'd help his family make a move from they were living in a mobile home at the edge of the city. Their plan was to move into something nicer in a more established community. Despite the opportunity to make a commission I decided to say no. It was one of my first attempts to say no to a potential commission cheque and to a family member.

The most important reason to say no to my relative was practical: I did not feel the sale of a mobile home was aligned with my desired brand and the brand I was developing. Knowing what you are about and what brand you want to represent is a critical first step in building a business.

It wasn't that I was better than the opportunity. At the time, I would wear one of the two suits I owned almost every day and I was driving a borrowed BMW. I wanted to appear as a more experienced version of myself when I was dealing with my ideal demographic. I had decided I would rather spend my time sitting open houses for other agents in the inner-city than learning how to work the mobile trailer business.

Saying no only comes after you've said yes a thousand times. Finding clarity takes time and this was one of the moments where I started to see clearly where I wanted to go.

Although initially my family member struggled with my response, my decision to keep our personal and work lives separate may have helped protect the strong relationship we have now. Saying no can open doors too, it turns out.

The ability to say no has been valuable for me over the past decade. On every phone call, email or sales call, I do my best to use my trained intuition and a structured set of questions to determine if the potential client is a fit for our business. It's no longer about saying yes to everything.

Be careful not to get too excited about saying no, though. There are times I've had to push past an initial no reaction. Taking the extra time to get past my first impression has led to some of the best clients I've had.

Don't let a snap judgment get in the way of curiosity. Seek input from your team. Get clear before you close a door.

THE FIRST TIME I WALKED AWAY FROM $1 MILLION

I think most people are pleasers by nature. Personally, I find it feels better to say yes than it does to say no. Growing up I always thought a no represented failure.

The first time I said no to $1 million in seed capital, I did it because I was following my gut.

I knew it was my gut because matters of the gut always involve intense feelings of joy or sadness. Think back to when you last met someone amazing or discovered someone you trusted had been dishonest. That feeling was your gut communicating.

Feelings are important indicators to me. Just like traffic lights, different feelings cause me to react in different ways.

Nerves are feelings I've been able to use throughout my life.

Just say no to always saying yes

They help me identify times when something life-altering is about to happen that requires me to act. They're like spidey senses.

Fear, on the other hand, is an unpredictable feeling.

Then there's the feeling of doubt. When the American real estate market crashed in 2008, the timing and circumstances seemed too good to ignore. Along with some business partners, I started a company that targeted distressed U.S. real estate assets. We had done our due diligence, secured a couple of assets under contract, and I had gotten a Nexus card so I could be back and forth across the border a few times a month without wasting time at the airport. Everything seemed to be falling into place nicely.

Then I set out to raise capital. That process also seemed to be going perfectly. People believed in me and our company's business plan. I had money in the bank and commitments on paper. Then one of my biggest commitments came through and offered up $1 million.

That is when my gut instinct kicked in.

Despite the signs that seemed to suggest the opposite, I had an impossible to ignore seed of doubt in my gut. It wasn't fear or nerves; I could tell the difference. It was an intense feeling of doubt. Your gut doesn't care about your ego, which is why you can trust it.

I did all I needed to do internally and externally to qualify the feeling, to make sure it was really doubt and not just indigestion. The end result was I walked into my business partner's office on a Sunday, ended the business relationship and broke up with the company. I didn't accept the million-dollar investment. I did it all with tears in my eyes. And did I mention it was my business partner's birthday? My gut was right and we were wrong about our timing.

Years later, I can say that we were amongst the smartest guys in the business because we walked away. We were speculating more than we were calculating in our moves and there was more uncertainty than was worth gambling on.

Truth is, I just had a feeling. And I think it's a feeling we all get.

Entrepreneurs know which feelings mean slam the brakes and which mean accelerate.

Don't ignore your gut. Understand which feelings are the real ones.

You'll know them by the heart-wrenching, gut-churning and tear-jerking that comes from making the tough decisions. As a decision-maker of any sort, you'll learn it can be very painful to make a decision—like saying no to $1 million in seed capital or doing essential layoffs. But that pain means it's the right decision.

Trust your gut.

SAY NO WITH GRACE

As a growing business, how you say no is critical. Although I wouldn't recommend doing it with tears, I do recommend doing it sincerely.

Never say no with arrogance.

Think of it this way. Trendy new restaurants build themselves up from zero diners to a lineup out the door. The problem I consistently see is they don't know how to turn away people gracefully.

Some restaurants offer a glass of wine and a callback service. Others—the majority of others that I've experienced in our city—have staff who do it with a dash of pompousness. A sort of, "Please piss off and don't come back because we don't need to be any busier."

I tried to order a takeout salad the other night from one of my favourite restaurants. Not only did I have to call a few times to get an answer, but the person on the line advised me it would take two hours for the salad. I pointed out that I had only ordered a salad. A salad! He said, "Do you have any idea how busy we are?" Given I was calling from my cellphone, my answer was obviously no.

A glass of wine or a flippant response? One tells your customers you don't care about them and the other will make a massive difference in your business' growth.

Stay humble.

Hustle hard.

Be thankful.

WHEN THEY SAY NO TO YOU, DON'T TAKE IT PERSONALLY

There's a big difference between making a business relationship personal, and taking the outcomes of the experience personally. You should definitely make it personal, but don't ever take it personally.

I always seek to understand why anyone chooses not to work with me. Some entrepreneurs take offence or turn the blame for a missed opportunity on the other party. I seek to learn from my mistakes in an effort to gain something from every relationship, even if it's just a better understanding of my failures.

One of my first questions when a potential client chooses to interview me is one that allows me to understand what their past real estate experience was like. I've often asked, "Have you worked with a real estate agent in the past and what didn't you like about that experience?" Their answer would give me massive insight into what they didn't want to experience again. After all, it was me at the table, not their last real estate agent, which meant there was likely something in the past interaction that caused the sales rep not to be invited back to the client's table.

That one loaded question opened the door to a tremendous amount of learning for me. The question has since evolved. The initial question was about fact-finding and learning what not to do in my business. Now I also ask, "What is it about your past real estate experience that you enjoyed?" I learn what worked before and what we should do to make this the best experience possible.

These questions also allow me to know early on if the client is hoping for service I can live up to. "Under-promise and over-deliver," may be a cliché, but you can only achieve it if you know what the client's expectations are.

I wasn't always this mature about feedback. After all, I'm human. Not taking things personally takes practice. Expect it to take a few wins before you can view failures as beneficial.

One of the first times I took a business failure personally was the day I was driving to my exam to receive my real estate licence. On the way to my exam, I passed by my best friend's mom's house and saw a new "For sale" sign on her lawn.

I was devastated. She knew I was about to start my business and would likely struggle in the beginning. The experience and revenue that would come from her sales process would benefit me hugely.

I called her right away and asked why she didn't trust me to sell her house. Her answer was simple: I was just too new. The sale of her home was the biggest business transaction she would have ever been involved in. It included lots of moving parts that required experience I simply didn't have yet.

I thought the fact we were so close would be my in, but our closeness allowed her to fully understand my weaknesses. This woman knew nearly everything about me, not just the professional brand I was promoting.

When I got over the initial pain, I found a lesson. In this industry, you need to keep your brand professional, hold your head high and always exit gracefully. Yes, sales is about relationships, caring and sharing. But while being a kind ear can help define you as trustworthy, there's no need for you to reveal all to a client early on, too.

Despite my gut reaction to be upset, I did hold my head high. I supported her decision and moved onto my first sale. And my second and third and fourth sale.

And a few months into my new real estate business, her listing came to me. And I sold it.

CHAPTER 8

Building a database

"Six degrees of separation doesn't mean that everyone is linked to everyone else in just six steps. It means that a very small number of people are linked to everyone else in a few steps, and the rest of us are linked to the world through those special few."

—Malcolm Gladwell,
author

THE LIFEBLOOD OF SALES
IS YOUR DATABASE

Some say you're only as good as your next sale. I say a salesperson is only as good as his or her database, how up to date the database is and how truly connected the salesperson is with everybody on that list. Your database is really your last sale and how well you honour that sale. More literally, your database is the list of people you have relationships with, who know who you are and what you offer, and who are willing to maintain a relationship with you that revolves around your business.

A good database will consist of a wide variety of people, all at different stages of the sales relationship, all with the potential to influence your business.

Above all else, a sign of a great database is one that consists of people who you could pick up the phone to call on any given day and, importantly, have it not be awkward.

If you can't do that, then you need to work on the people in your database. This is also the difference between having a database and a contact list. The vast majority of sales, good business and great life events will happen from a database.

Before you can sell to the people in your database, you will have to connect with them and, most likely, need to meet them or at minimum talk to them on the phone. Unfortunately, a database isn't a product you can purchase or find laying around. You may inherit it from someone else if you're lucky, but even then, it's not your database until you build relationships with everyone on the list. One at a time.

THERE IS NO SHORTCUT TO BUILDING A DATABASE

Your database will be a reflection of the work and time you put into it.

Initially, your database will be small. It begins as a simple list of those you know have the potential to buy from you. Think friends, family, past business contacts and peers. Essentially anyone who will listen to you talk and consider what you have to offer.

Even if they don't buy, your initial database will give you the opportunity to practice your pitch and communicate your value. In fact, it's better to practice on those who know you well. In my experience, those people have the tendency to tell you some of the hard truths you'll need to hear about your weaknesses and your pitch.

Your ability to both recognize and leverage the people and resources that surround you will be the difference between ultimate success and failure.

You'll notice that I said "will be" and not "could be." I cannot stress enough how in sales, and business in general, you are always on stage. Your ability to connect with others will be the only factor differentiating you and thousands of others just like you.

For me when I started out in sales, it was about recognizing who was closest to me at the time and how I could best connect with them. What did they need from me, how could I be of assistance and where were there opportunities for us to work together?

Your existing resources stretch further than just those who know your last name. Remember that introductions can be hard to come by when networking, so stretch your mind to include anyone you have met: schools, past jobs, parents' friends, friends' parents, teammates, neighbours and your entire social media database.

Once I had exhausted the opportunities that already existed around me, I started doing the only thing I could to get my name out: I made calls. Lots of calls. Pots and pans sales required 20 to 30 cold calls a day to get a single sale.

When I started working in real estate, my database options were minimal. I had a few people I'd met during my years in pots and pans sales, and I'd met a lot of people over the years who would take a call from their old friend Dennis. But I needed more.

I started building a database in a time where social media and email contact lists didn't exist. I had a three-inch-thick municipal phonebook, my personal address book and whatever business cards I had managed to collect over the years.

So that's exactly where I started.

I had recently gotten married and had a list of names and addresses for all the guests. I sent them each a letter. Not an email either, a handwritten letter, followed by a phone call to almost every guest.

It took months to get responses and make connections. Most of the calls and letters did not lead to sales, but that didn't mean they weren't part of my database. I made sure to touch base with everyone who was willing to answer my calls in an attempt to groom them into future clients. Things didn't happen immediately. I was having plenty of conversations and preparing for the marathon. Calls equal conversations equal coffee meetings equal lunch meetings, which in the end equal sales.

What can you do if you don't start with a list of contacts? Lots.

I have a friend who is very successful in sales. He started off with even fewer contacts than I had. His approach to building his database was to simply go where people were to meet them. He would join every club, group, community, organization and society that would have him. From learning to knit to roller derby, he would be there meeting people and building relationships.

To me, the best part was he'd found a way to get his foot in the door conversationally simply by having things in common with each group.

If these approaches sound long and tedious, that's because they are.* But if we could do it using handwritten letters and cold call introductions, imagine how much easier it is to do it in today's digitally driven age. The same rules apply to building the database, but maintaining it has become a little easier.

One of the hardest things to get over when building your database is the fear of calling. I completely understand this. I take for granted how much fun I think cold calling is, but I'm reminded of its reality for most people every time I go out with a new associate. Picking up the phone to call somebody you haven't spoken to in a while or knocking on their door is difficult. But please remember: just as you feel guilty for not connecting with them, they feel as guilty for not getting in touch with you.

If the relationship is going to have substance, and if it is one of the relationships that has the potential to grow, then the meeting will go well. If it's not meant to be then just touch base and exit quickly.

---

* A great tool for building a database is Tom Ferry's ABCs of building a database. A PDF is available on his website. He's impacted my business massively over the years.

In real estate today, my team has a database target that increases by 50 to 100 people annually. Currently we are at about 1,000 people our team needs to personally contact yearly. We have a warm database of about 500. The calls are essential both to maintain the database and to grow it organically.

In addition, each salesperson must call each of their own contacts and direct connections annually. Conversations are what lead to sales. The more conversations, the more sales.

CHAPTER 9

Perception matters more than reality

"You cannot climb the ladder of success dressed in the costume of failure."

–Zig Ziglar,
author, motivational speaker

LOOK THE PART

Sales is a lot like dating: you're willing to give more to people you connect with. The challenge with sales is that you're often in competition with others who offer similar value for the chance to connect. With so many salespeople vying for the attention of the same audience, one single negative impression can be enough to eliminate you from the shortlist. Don't give it to them.

One of the best compliments my team can get from a prospective buyer or seller is if, at the end of the meeting they ask, "So, are you taking new clients right now?" We want them to want us so badly they aren't sure they qualify. That's only possible when you make the first impression the best it can be.

Again, like dating, the first impression can be enough to get you in the door, or it could get that door slammed in your face.

This is why I advise anyone in sales to always look the part.

In sales "looking the part" is not a universal look. It's not cufflinks or a Mercedes, but it could be. It could also be flip-flops, a parka or a cowboy hat. The only thing to consider when choosing how you will look the part is: what does my audience value?

Obviously, what they value will go beyond the clothes you wear or the car you drive, but a consideration of these things will help you with your first impression, and in sales, that's often the only impression you get to make.

Before you will ever have the chance to prove yourself with your actions, you have a huge opportunity to tell your story with the first impression you leave.

Whether I was working as a DJ, selling pots and pans, or in real estate, the BMW, suit, glasses, apron and purple spandex Speedo* all served the purpose of presenting me well during a first impression because I knew my audience before I showed up.

When I first started in the pots and pans business I wasn't much of a cook. I liked to cook and had experience in a couple of restaurants, but going from deep-frying fish and chips to putting on an eight-course meal with pots and pans that cost thousands of dollars, all while trying to close a sale, was a completely new and very challenging experience.

---

* I competed in a few natural bodybuilding competitions when I was young and good-looking. One of the requirements was posing in a Speedo. This was shocking for everyone I had invited to the event, especially my dad who hadn't seen me in years and didn't recognize me.

This is where preparation comes in. Whether it is cooking dinners or selling houses, the event is not the important part; the conversations are. Doing as much meal preparation as possible in advance ensured I could focus on the talking rather than the cooking. For showing houses, it's about previewing and knowing exactly what route we will be taking so I'm not looking for a map when I should be looking in the client's eyes.

In addition to preparing food for dinner shows, I prepared my appearance and my supplies. I would show up with a shiny set of cookware packed in the nicest green Samsonite suitcase and a red Coleman cooler full of ingredients. This equipment choice matched the red or blue apron I would wear (given to me by my grandmother-from-another-mother Hanna) to help me look like I knew what I was doing.

I had some of the best sales collateral possible. I used a binder with full-colour brochures featuring health facts and all of the comparables required to build a compelling case for the cookware. It was all rounded out by a half-decent meal.

The most important ingredients in the entire dinner show were practice and Betty Crocker icing. I practiced on friends and family often. I used my cookware at home all the time. I read all of the collateral I could get my hands on to ensure that when I showed up for a dinner show, I didn't just look the part. I was prepared.

WHY MY FACE ISN'T ON A BUS BENCH

When I moved from pots and pans to the real estate business, I continued to do my best to look the part for each and every call.

I had what some may refer to as a "baby face" and I never exactly made up for it with size. I'm forced to resort to stature and attitude to capture attention and build trust. When that doesn't work, I stand on a phone book.

When starting out, I looked especially young when compared to the average 57-year-old Realtor. In an industry where experience means everything, first impressions can be the difference between a $10,000 payday and paying bills with a credit card.

Let's face it. People are judging machines wrapped in skin.

I rarely use my photo on sales collateral. I made the mistake early on of thinking I was handsome enough to put my photo on my business cards. Unless you're selling your beauty or body, your face on an ad hurts more than it helps.

Plus, kids love to draw moustaches on ads, and I look awful in a moustache.

Yet, in my industry putting faces on collateral is rampant. There are more bus benches with real estate people's heads on them than any other business. In fact, I don't think there is an industry that exists where people get paid as much as we do and all they really do is promote themselves: their head, their award status, their cool slogan, and how beautiful or sophisticated they appear.

Putting your picture on your bus bench, billboard or business card is a mistake. The problem with having your photo on anything is, as it's your first impression, it will allow the prospect to make up an entire story about you without even meeting you. Right or wrong, they will do this. They are doing it right now. Embrace the reality; it's not paranoia.

Unless you have a well-oiled and very expensive marketing firm that's going to ensure your brand is well-represented and held in the utmost regard, your face will most likely disqualify you more than it qualifies you.

Even if you are blessed with beauty, this will scare more people away than it attracts. A beautiful saleswoman may cause the husband to call, but it could upset his wife and, well ... good luck after that.

There is something about having grey hair that says experience. But not to everybody. Somebody who has grey hair may not appeal to a younger audience; somebody who looks younger may not appeal to an older audience.

Glasses, a tie, bright lipstick, colourful clothes. All of it may help or hurt a first impression, but those things don't represent 100% of who you are. Keep your face off of things to eliminate the opportunity for a customer to disqualify you as a competent service provider prior to meeting face to face.

Once you're face to face, if you're good enough, you can

overcome any superficial obstacles with your professional skills. Remember though, it could be the superficial objections you present that prevent you from getting the appointment in the first place.

Perception matters more than reality. I knew that when I was a cute, scared, kid smiling and saying "please" and "thank you," and I know now that optics and sales are massively correlated.

Let me repeat that, as I think it was one of the most important concepts I've discovered in my business.

Perception matters more than reality.

THE CAR MATTERS

When I was picking up a new buyer or seller early on, I always looked the part. This meant I needed to borrow my mother-in-law's BMW. I polished it right before picking up a client once. I thought he was one of the most well-dressed people I'd ever met. The first thing he said when I picked him up was he liked my car and appreciated the way I kept it in such impeccable condition.

Later, I ended up selling him one of my first million-dollar condos and I've since received several referrals from him. The car didn't get me the sale. The car kept the door open long enough for me to sell myself. Still, I'm grateful to him for causing me to be a little obsessive compulsive about how clean I keep my car. Win-win, I think.

I think most real estate agents drive fancy cars, but it's something I have since learned to modify according to the buyer or seller I'm meeting.

I know one real estate agent who has an arsenal of different vehicles he chooses from when meeting different clients. There are times you won't want to look as though you're living in the lap of luxury when your income comes in the form of commission on your client's sales. And there may be other times you need to rent a driver and a Mercedes. Based on the fact this agent was one of the Top 5 in the world, I would suggest a part of what he does works for him.

But it's not as simple as having the best of everything, because the image that gets you the sale in the city may backfire elsewhere.

I first met a now-longstanding client after being invited to meet about a property that I knew two icons of real estate were bidding against me to represent. I won his business and I was seriously curious what made him choose me over two guys with more experience, connections and stature. So I asked. His response was simple: "Did you see the Porsche that guy drove up in? He either charges too much or is far too busy to give my property the attention it deserves."

I'm not saying we need to be deceptive. I'm saying we need to be aware first impressions matter, and in this industry, business may or may not happen based simply because of the car you pull up in.

I have resolved that as my vehicle is an extension of my office, to always have a spacious, clean and professional-looking vehicle as a means of instilling confidence, without showing off. This is my way of making both upper-end, high-net-worth individuals and first-time buyers comfortable. I aim to make the passenger's seat as comfortable as my foyer or living room.

To this end, my team makes a habit of calling buyers or sellers prior to meeting to learn their preferred Starbucks beverage so we can have it available in the vehicle when they get in. If nothing else, we will always have snacks and chilled bottles of water. It's all about making a great first impression. People are expecting professionals to show up. Let them know they are getting the best of the best before you even open your mouth.

DRESS FOR THE COMFORT OF YOUR AUDIENCE

Instilling confidence in a prospect is essential to getting a sale and it starts the moment you meet them.

One of the problems we're experiencing today is a lot of the next generation, although incredibly brilliant, talented and creative, have chosen to really just be who they are. By this I mean they will show up for work in sneakers, blue jeans and dreadlocks. Although I understand and support the need to be an individual, I don't think it's a good sales strategy. You need to meet your audience where they're at. Whether pitching to a boardroom full of executives or a farmer looking to sell his ranch, it's important to satisfy their need for comfort, and to avoid as many avenues of doubt as possible during the first impression.

I dress for success every time I leave the house. I'm not saying I wear a Boss suit every day. I dress according to the appointments I have set for the day.

Most days it's a nicely pressed suit, but some days it's hiking boots and blue jeans. Evaluating a multimillion-dollar condo versus a ranch requires different "costumes," if you will.

I didn't always follow my own advice. Like many life lessons, I learned the importance of my appearance the hard way.

For the first few years I worked in the real estate industry I tried my best to not wear a suit. I was Dennis: a cool and casual, fist-bumping charm machine who figured wearing my heart on my sleeve made for appropriate attire in any situation. I had been attracted to the freedom offered by the real estate industry and the successful real estate agents I knew all seemed pretty casual. I followed their lead.

One day, I found a pair of slip-on, slip-off Croc-style dress shoes at a department store. I thought to myself, "These are perfect for someone always coming in and out of houses." Plus they were "cool" and "unique"—just like Dennis.

So I rocked those clunky bad boys out to a listing

appointment. Because of their loose fit, the clodhoppers were kind of clomping down the driveway as we examined the property. I'll never forget the client stopping short and looking down at my feet with a look of half-disgust and half-pity.

"Where'd ya get them fancy shoes, son?"

I'm sure he thought I looked like an idiot. And I must have. Here he is discussing trusting me with arguably the biggest sales transaction of his life, and I am showing him I can't even be trusted to handle a simple shoe purchase.

Disregard the claim that no one looks at a man's shoes. They'll look when they're the wrong shoes. I don't always know what call or meeting I have that will be the most important of the day, but I do my best to dress for my audience. It's better to be unnecessarily prepared than caught with the wrong shoes on.

Eventually I figured out I should be wearing my best suit as often as possible. I wore pressed dress shirts every day and always carried a blazer in my car. I would go so far as to wear non-prescription glasses to help me look more sophisticated.

I got rid of my spiky blonde highlights and went with a more traditional parted look for my haircut. In fact, the age and demographic of the prospect I am meeting has even influenced the hairstyle I choose for the day.

We need to meet people where they're at. Feeling comfortable as a presenter is essential. Getting rid of the opportunity for the prospect to have conversations in their head about anything other than what you're trying to sell is critical. Minimize the noise and rein in their attention.

BE AS PREPARED AS YOU LOOK

All of that said, you can never show up looking the part, driving the right car or having the right hair while being ill-prepared. Do your homework on every front. Know your prospect, their needs, expectations, desires, fears and the journey you will be taking them on.

Be prepared. Preparation plus presentation can trump everything else, especially when the stakes are high. It's not all about image. Never underestimate the power of being prepared.

In addition to doing our homework, we'll often send a digitally tracked pre-meeting package. It's a custom-designed professional information kit, highlighting our team and the benefits the prospect would receive by working with us. We're notified when they open the attachment.

We will confirm the appointment prior to meeting, ensure they have received the materials and ask if they have had a chance to review them. Thanks to the digital tracking, we already know they have, and the timeliness of our follow-up ensures our several points of contact complement each other right up until the point of our pitch. All of this is intended to have them feeling satisfied before we enter their home or they enter the vehicle.

Our competitors who think the client experience starts after they arrive at the first face-to-face meeting are at a serious disadvantage. During the entire process, always, always, always be looking to build credibility. We don't get second chances to make first impressions.

You can never be overprepared for a sales call.

In fact, the individual who is overprepared rather than underprepared could show up in their underwear and could close the sale before the guy or girl in the nice suit driving the fancy car. It's not either/or, it's both/and.

HOW MUCH TRANSPARENCY IS TOO MUCH?

There is a time for transparency and the timing of it is crucial. Although I understand the importance of transparency in relationships, I don't feel it has much to do with first impressions. First off, I think the true definition of transparency and the implementation of it in regards to sales has gotten lost.

Transparency doesn't mean saying and doing whatever we feel like. I think it's about saying and doing what is ultimately best for the individual you are being transparent with.

Let me give you an example. While I did my best to make my appearance the very best it could be as a professional, I went down a path in 2009 that inevitably caused my brand to suffer.

I went into video blogging.

Early video blogging was a form of marketing that resulted from the convenient use of flip cameras and smartphone devices. Seemingly overnight it became one of the easiest ways to promote and share ideas.

Notice that I said "promote and share" rather than "communicate." Sales is all about communication. The problem with video blogging, although it's easy, convenient and scalable, is that it's one-sided.

There was really no conversation to be had. Although I liked the idea, I missed the very important reality that all I was doing was telling, not communicating. Sales is about uncovering problems and then recommending solutions. The solutions should be customized to the problems of the individual.

I didn't just video blog casually. I became a video-blogging maniac.

I recorded close to 100 episodes in a few short months. They were high-energy, risky and often touched on controversial topics within the industry. In fact, one of my first episodes almost got me sued. I had called out a real estate agent by name. Although what I said happened to be the truth, it wasn't the right way to communicate that truth. It wasn't two-way. It wasn't a conversation. It wasn't a way that he could be heard in rebuttal.

In the same way, when we post videos of ourselves, we're not inviting other people into the dialogue. We're not inviting ourselves into their living rooms. We're really just talking at them.

Don't get me wrong. It was fun. I recorded the very first episode in the basement of my house with the background music of Public Enemy. The song was Don't Believe the Hype, and I was talking about the hype of real estate.

It was a good idea, and one that could have been entertaining, were it not for my extremely bad execution.

I was known at the time as a bit of a luxury brand; an up-and-coming rock star in real estate. Then these videos started to show up.

As I mentioned, I didn't just stumble into it. I was in a full-on sprint to be the biggest and most well-known video blogger around. Well, I succeeded, sort of. I became quite known in real estate circles locally and was invited to speak at several events. It felt great to be invited to share. Almost like I actually knew something.

In hindsight, I think people were just curious about how a guy like me, being as goofy as I was on video, could be pulling this off and actually still selling houses.

In addition to recording a few videos a week, I was sending them directly to my entire database. For some reason, I believed they just had to see what I was doing. My intentions were good. I was being creative and providing important real estate information. The problem is nobody wants unsolicited rants thrown at them, and they especially don't want it yelled at them.

A big breakthrough for me came when one of my dearest friends sat me down and asked me an important question about my video blogging. He said, "Dennis, what the hell are you doing?"

He was essentially saying that I was known as being a hardworking, very personal and skilled real estate rock star and the videos were not telling that story.

My business had dropped over the few months that I was aggressively video blogging.

It was just confusing for clients. When I noticed that my business was starting to flag, I polled a few important clients and mentors. I did what I should've done earlier on: I asked them for their opinion. Most of them said they loved it. Then I asked a key question: "Would you use the video blogs to recommend me or connect me with any of your friends and family who are thinking of selling?"*

(Imagine a long, pregnant pause.)

"Probably not."

First impressions matter most.

Pulling up in a clean, respectable vehicle with a suit on and having all of your shit together is probably a better way to go.

---

* This, by the way, is the single most important question we can ask of anyone that's in our sphere of influence when it comes to our marketing.

DON'T #SHARE TOO MUCH

It can be tough to keep a handle on sharing in a world that's so obsessed with it. Social media provides a tool that oversharers use daily and, whether they know it or not, they potentially disqualify themselves from working relationships with their audiences.

You don't have to look far for a news story that covers someone's fall from grace via an unpopular or offensive post that went viral and trumpeted their doom in the courts of public perception.

Oversharing doesn't have to go viral to cause damage to your brand.

Stay professional and keep your posts clean and acceptable for all ages. It's that simple.

One small but golden rule I use on social media is in regards to holidays and downtime. I rarely post pictures online of myself on vacation, having fun or doing anything that doesn't involve work until way after the fact. Avoid the perception that all you do is take holidays and have fun and you'll avoid any problems that might arise from it. The exception is if having crazy adventures and being the centre of fun is part of your brand. If, for example, you're a Red Bull rep or selling GoPro cameras, then by all means, make sure that's reflected in what you share. But for more conventional salespeople, we need to keep it professional.

Keep hustling and make that apparent in your online profiles.

One-on-one business meetings need to be personal. Discussing personal information ensures the meeting has significance. However, our public brand and the public's perception of our brand needs to be as solid and as professional as possible. It's especially true when working in a sector of the marketplace that is high net worth. Real estate is no exception. Given the significance of the transactions for clients and the sums of money they invest to engage the services of real estate agents our brand needs to be professional.

Perception matters more than reality.

LEARN TO DRINK

Acting the part is much easier to do if you're not intoxicated.

I seldom drink at functions. And when I say "drink," I mean have more than one or two drinks. Unless it's Las Vegas, two drinks is my limit.

The truth is "I used to be too good at it." The double-edged sword of my personality is that I tend to take things to the extreme. I don't do anything half-assed. I get easily inspired and next thing I know I'm chasing a new passion head-on with reckless abandon. So I am selective about the activities and commitments I engage in.

I was not always this selective, and at one point in my life one of my more ill-advised passions included recreational drinking.

In and around the time when most of my friends were going to university, I liked to party. I became, in my own mind, one of the best entertainers and partiers in our crowd. I was a lot of fun to be around and I have the scars and missing teeth to prove it (circa a Tragically Hip mosh pit in 1998).

The good news for me is this was before smartphones and Facebook. It was also just before I became serious about going after what I wanted in life. A lot of friends I had around that time have become clients today.

Regardless of what age or stage you're at, you are always building relationships and your reputation. And because of today's technology, you can be guaranteed there will exist, for this generation and every one in the foreseeable future, a permanent record of the horrible and beautiful decisions you make.

There was something about the way I grew up and the way that my mother raised me. I have always been mindful, and in many ways self-conscious, about my reputation.

Thankfully, this resulted in good governance for most of the decisions I made as a young person. Unless I was adding alcohol to the decision. As I grew in my career and found the direction I wanted my life to go, I began to drink less and party less. At one point I gave up alcohol completely.

This proved to be a bit of a problem as I entered the business scene. When I joined a business forum of like-minded entrepreneurs, I was the youngest and least-successful guy in attendance. We would often go together to conferences and out-of-town retreats where we grew up together as salespeople.

In my eyes, each of these guys was significantly more sophisticated and wiser than I was. I can't possibly tell you in this short book how much I learned and grew because of the influence each of them had on my life. The lessons ranged from how to manage a marriage, to raising kids, to growing a business. All of them were ahead of me in each of these areas and all of them had so much to teach.

It was on one of our retreats that one of the individuals pointed out to me that my zero-tolerance attitude towards alcohol may be a hindrance to my ability to build relationships. He said having a drink or two might be a good thing to consider.

This was in no way a peer pressure move or bravado-driven taunt. This was practical advice. In certain circles and meetings, having a social drink may earn social equity. It's also true that people who don't drink can respond poorly to alcohol when they do imbibe.

Should it be this way? Do you have to go along with it? How much of a difference does it make? Everyone will have their own answers to these questions. Sometimes we need to compromise, sometimes we will want to, sometimes we decide not to. Choose your own battles.

For my part, I decided this is one area where I chose to adapt rather than resist. Not only did I learn to drink occasionally and professionally, but I decided to build enough tolerance that I could maintain composure while drinking socially and stay on my game at all times.

In 2005 I had the opportunity to go to China to study the culture, language and tactics within the real estate sector. It was a four-and-a-half-month journey where we visited more than 30 cities. We attended business meetings, toured factories and were hosted by politicians and business leaders.

I learned quickly that drinking alcohol was going to be a non-negotiable part of the meetings we would be attending. Part of this was due to the fairly young average age of our group. There were 13 of us, all in our early 20s. Wherever we toured, we'd be paired with the young staff within the company. After the first few meetings we learned we needed a designated drinker.

The designated drinker would take a toast when our cheerful hosts proposed one. And they seemed to want to toast everything. Instead of everyone drinking constantly, our designated drinker would stand to be the centre of attention and take one for the team. Literally.

China is serious about business, and Chinese business-people are just as serious about getting to know you. Developing rapport and engaging in meaningful small talk is a major part of their business customs, and what better way to do this than to throw a party. The subtle motive was after a few drinks certain people tend to speak more than others; probably more than they should.

As they say, "Loose lips sink ships," and loose lips fuelled with Baijiu can sink reputations and even corporations.

Alcohol is the great equalizer. I witnessed this first-hand playing music for Christmas parties and weddings as part of my early business as a DJ. I can't possibly count the many disasters I witnessed. One guy decided to drop his pants during a colourful, impromptu and unappreciated dance to Rasputin. He woke up the next day without a job.

I was thankfully only an observer to such situations, and learned the advantages of being the conscious observer in life compared to an intoxicated participant. It takes a lifetime to build a reputation, but it can be broken in a matter of seconds.

Now, I'm a pragmatist. A glass of wine, good scotch or cold beer will move a conversation further, faster. It helps get business done. It's just part of the deal.

I closed my biggest pots and pans sale ever over some homemade brew with Eli at the Hutterite colony. More recently, I've negotiated some of my biggest real estate deals over a glass of wine. I cannot say the same thing about iced tea or apple juice.

CHAPTER 10

Say less & listen more: rocking meetings

"Better to be silent and be thought a fool than to speak and remove all doubt."

–Abraham Lincoln

BE MORE INTERESTED
THAN INTERESTING

I rarely carry business cards. As a sales guy, this may seem counterintuitive. I get that. But the truth is very few people ever follow up with real estate people. We can often be the most uninteresting people in the room.

When someone reaches to shake your hand and asks what you do at a party they're often looking for a reason to move onto the next, more interesting person in the room.

Instead of giving out my card, I collect others' contact information. Collecting business cards—or putting information straight into your cellphone—ensures you'll be able to follow up with those who are truly interesting and show them you are more interested than the average real estate agent. You can't expect them to be the ones who reach out to you.

One situation with the potential to make or break your

ability to appear professional is how you act in a meeting or at a party. Whether the meeting is at a coffee shop, cocktail party, over Skype or in a boardroom, how you act will tell a lot about you as a person and professional service provider.

Far too often I meet salespeople who feel the need to fill every second of available time with talk, often repeating things in a redundant manner or covering topics that have nothing to do with the point of the meeting. They're just filling silence.

The 17th-century French mathematician Blaise Pascal once wrote, "I would have written a shorter letter, but I did not have the time." It remains relevant hundreds of years later. The idea being that the best-presented thoughts require consideration in order to be delivered in a concise and valuable way.

It's human nature to talk more when we lack confidence. The silence heightens our feelings of inadequacy. The inexperienced individual thinks they will distract from their lack of knowledge by keeping their audience's ears filled with, well, anything.

In sales this is a big mistake.

In my experience, whoever says the least in a negotiation tends to win. The stories vary, but one message remains consistent: after the pitch is made, whoever speaks first, loses.

In sales, quiet confidence is paramount. We all have experience with the strong and silent type. The man or woman who doesn't need to talk loudly or often to be respected or feared. Their actions, image and reputation speak volumes on their behalf.

We've all also had more than enough experience with the opposite situation. That loud-mouthed, fast-talking, untrustworthy friend or colleague who gabs like he's selling used cars, fitting as many idioms and exaggerations into the mix as possible to distract from the lack of substance in his product. You just get the feeling that even though he won't stop talking, he isn't telling you anything you can use.

In sales, the ability to pick your message's timing, based on intimate knowledge of a client's situation, will reap the most advantageous results.

In sales you will find yourself in two types of meetings. The first is the most common: you are there to learn. You are not the smartest person in the room. You are there to catch up your knowledge to the level held by other participants.

The other type of meeting is one where you find yourself thinking you already know everything being discussed. If you find yourself in that type of meeting most of the time, then it's time to analyze the meetings you are booking. In sales, we should be going to very few meetings where we already know everything being discussed.

There are two types of people in any meeting: those there to learn as much as they can and those who are wasting everyone's time. When you are in sales and attending meetings you need to find yourself in the first category most of the time. Be interested rather than trying to prove you're interesting. Even when you do know that you know more than anyone in the room, make sure you ask thoughtful questions and only offer very valuable nuggets of your own feedback. Save the rest for later.

Being more interested than interesting can translate into sales.

Practice fine-tuning your message and know your product and industry better than anyone else. For every sales call, meeting, interview, presentation or whatever, make sure you are prepared.

Do your homework and bring more than what is required. Just showing up won't cut it. Know what you are going to say and make sure you have spent time figuring out the best way to say it. This means writing it down, understanding what it means to both you and your audience and practicing it until you are confident.

For the most part, any statements you deliver in a meeting should be derived from the questions you have been asking. Knowing your information is important, but knowing the questions you're going to ask and how you're going to ask them is essential too.

My favourite example of this comes from stand-up comedy. A few years ago I had the opportunity to meet a local celebrity. He was one of the most sought-after comedians, MCs and TV personalities in the business.

Over lunch I asked him how he did it. How was it that for every show he did or audience he was in front of he seemed to knock it out of the park? He told me there's never just one way to go. He said he starts every stand-up show by asking a few questions to learn about his audience. ("By applause, anyone here from out of town?" "How about those election results?" and the like.) From there he would take the show in the direction that best suited the audience.

Brilliant. Ask questions and then take them on the ride of their lives.

FINDING CONFIDENCE IN MEETINGS

Once you are confident that what you know is correct, clear and of value, then hit the gas. Remember to provide additional information only when it is specific. Give only relevant answers aimed at instilling confidence.

Above all else, ensure your communication comes from a place of curiosity. Don't feel you need to use statements to sell, because what most clients will want to know, even more than what you know, is how invested you are in truly understanding what they want.

Be curious.

It seems simple enough, and yet so few of us do it.

I once watched a fresh hire arrive at all their meetings

concerned only with looking valuable. This person, like most of us in a new environment, felt everyone would be aware of how new and susceptible to mistakes they must be, and felt a need to prove their worth.

That isn't necessary. The act of getting the meeting is how you know you have already proven value to them.

In my industry, the fact we are licensed real estate agents shows we belong in the room, so we should be able to relax. Proving yourself as a professional is never the point of a meeting. The point of meeting a potential client is to prove to them your fit as an individual. The best way to convince others you're a fit isn't to tell them why, it's to ask them how.

Treat meetings like a test drive. You aren't in the vehicle to determine if it is in fact a car—a quick look at its outside and the fact that you are at a car dealership makes that pretty obvious. Rather, the test drive is to show you the unique characteristics of the specific car to ensure it is the best fit for your needs.

The real magic happens when the salesperson talks about your family and how they will fit in the car; the ages of your kids and the tools in the vehicle that will keep them happy; the cupholder for your coffee on the early drive to work; extra storage in the two additional glove compartments for your belongings; the extra outlets for the three cellphones he notices you're carrying.

Specific solutions to your specific problems is where the sale happens. Find those problems in your own prospects and offer solutions. Allowing the prospect to be in the driver's seat is the secret.

In the same way, those who come to meet with you are probably already aware of the services you offer or the position you hold and assume you're qualified to perform the duties they require. Why else would they meet with you?

Most meetings will not be about proving yourself as a professional, but rather, proving yourself as a good fit for the client's personality.

After you recite to them your polished pitch, relax. Now look for the right questions to ask to get you closer to the finish line you're shooting for.

BE A STRATEGIC QUESTIONER

Following your pitch, a potential client will ask follow-up questions if necessary, but chances are each question they ask will be loaded and attached to a need they have already identified.

For example, if they ask you about your hours of operation, what they might really be asking is, "Are you going to be available to address our needs when we need you? What restrictions on your time do you have?"

If you don't understand the nuance of the question, you may end up answering it in a way that doesn't relate to the client. Just as bad, you may realize there is more to this question than your hours and end up rambling, trying to cover every angle of the question in your response.

Either way, you can talk yourself out of the sale.

Rather than risk answering vague or loaded questions incorrectly, take control of the conversation and pull out the truth behind their veiled questions with some strategic interviewing of your own.

For example, when I ask about a client's past real estate experience, I use a particularly crafted question.

As I mentioned previously, I used to ask, "What didn't you like about your last real estate experience?" Now, I've rephrased it in the positive: "What did you like most?" The latter tends to naturally bring out the answer to the former, anyway.

The difference between the positive and negative framing of what may seem like the same question is subtle. But framing it in the positive has done three things:

1. It keeps me in control of the conversation.

2. It makes me look curious, but with their interests, not my own, in mind.

3. It gets me the answers I need to direct my actions.

I find the best strategy is to have a prepared list of questions aimed at uncovering the client's primary needs, concerns and objectives. Refer to this list often and take plenty of notes. Keep your questioning conversational, but keep it on track. You can also send your list of questions or a few basic questions prior to meeting. On my team, we have some basic scripts and questions we ask prior to each meeting, whether it be with buyers, sellers, builders or just general prospects.

These questions work as a filter to get us the information we need to excel in service of the client. It shows we have tuned into the client, and we've avoided rambling. Ideally, the client sees us as competent and a good fit.

You may be wondering how this can work if they're the one asking the questions. Let me assure you that without fail, 99% of the people you meet on Earth want to talk about themselves more than they want to talk about you. Period.

The problem with trying to satisfy a prospect's needs by answering questions is that the questions they ask aren't their real questions. We need to dig deeper to make sure we fully understand what they are asking and that they fully believe they are asking the right questions.

Once we are clear on the real questions being asked we can shape our answers to satisfy the concerns and solve any problems. Fact-finding and asking the right question is about finding the problems we as salespeople can agree to solve. If we can't solve the problem, then we may not want to agree to take on the business.

The strategy of talking less and listening more is not just for one-on-one meetings. In a group setting, where everyone fights for the chance to be heard and perceived as valuable, don't underestimate the benefits that come from quietly taking notes. Not only will this help you remember everything that went on in the meeting, giving you time to research anything you're still curious about or don't understand, it also makes those talking feel valued and heard.

Another challenge salespeople seem to trip over is the inability to take yes for an answer. Not knowing when to stop selling can turn an otherwise sold customer into someone annoyed their time is being wasted.

Learn to offer the opportunity for an answer to be given and then, if successful, shut up and leave. There is nothing more for you to do except start delivering on whatever they have said yes to.

In real estate, when a client says yes to working with us, it's like starting a journey together. Real estate transactions involve people, emotions, buying, selling and usually some seriously big changes in a person's life. Therefore, fact-finding and understanding a person's emotional state, their stated objectives and their unstated ones is essential.

Take in and write down as much as possible when you're learning from a client prior to starting the journey. It's a massive undertaking and it's different from going into a store to buy a product. Once you think you've heard enough to chart the course (and you think they have clearly articulated the course they want, too), shut up and start packing for the trip.

CHAPTER 11

Building a team

"The good news is that more than ever, value accrues to those that show up, those that make a difference, those that do work that matters."

—Seth Godin,
author

HIRING THE RIGHT PEOPLE

Eventually as a successful salesperson, you'll find the number of customers you're responsible to will become too big to manage alone. The all-important job of hiring the right people to maintain the high level of service you have attached to your brand becomes the challenge.

We can position ourselves to keep good things happening. My way of dealing with this is to acknowledge and celebrate my successes when they happen. This is essential to overcoming the fear that it was all "luck" and couldn't ever happen again. Instead of wondering what's around the next corner, I continue to put pressure on myself to perform at a higher level. I wake up a bit earlier, create better systems, stay at work a little later and have a few more conversations. I'll let you know how this plays out in another 10 years. For now it seems to be working pretty well.

I used to feel lucky in having amazing people around me and on my team. It seems like every assistant I get is even better than the last one. The truth is, it's not dumb luck. My team keeps getting better because I keep getting better about knowing my weaknesses and how I need to compensate. I've learned how to articulate my weaknesses as well as my strengths and how to be confident enough to do so. The more aware I can make the team about my weaknesses, the more likely I am to get support and the better we can all perform together.

Success attracts a lot of things. With growth, you have to be intentional about targeting successful individuals for your team. People with the right DNA. I have a rule: I'll always hire on potential and commitment over talent and a resume. Willingness trumps experience when building a team.

Sometimes a good team happens organically, but more often than not it's about smart selection. I haven't had to go far to make the selection on most occasions. Whenever possible, I hire people who are already close to my team's sphere of influence. Often friends or contacts of existing staff make excellent hires because we're able to understand a little about who they are beyond the person they showcase in interviews.

Chances are if they are staples in the lives of people already connected to our company, they will share the morals and professional beliefs we already have. They'll fit in on much more than a professional level; they will fit on a relationship level. Like attracts like.

When that isn't possible, and I have to rely largely on a job interview, I ask myself a simple, but important question: do I find this person interesting? If the answer is yes, then we've got a potential connection to build a future on.

Just like I prefer to do business with clients I can create a relationship with, I love working with people who are close to me. I think it helps for the simple fact that I can be a little crazy sometimes. I have more ideas than there are hours in a day and although I'm caffeinated most of the time, I really don't need it to be over-the-top excited.

If somebody can handle and appreciate this then we're off to a good start. If not, we probably shouldn't start at all.

Know who you are, where you are weak, where you want to go and find people who are willing to go with you.

HANDLING TIMES OF CHANGE

Dealing with me can be a challenge, as is often the case when a creative type is at the front of the parade. I am easily distracted and attracted to shiny objects.

One of my biggest strengths, which for a long time I thought was a weakness, is I change my mind often. I didn't think it was something leaders did. I thought commitment and decisiveness was important. I'm not sure when I started believing that, but lucky for me, Richard Branson in his book Losing My Virginity changed that.

He writes about being somebody who changes his mind frequently. He thinks it's something great leaders should do. I totally get it now. I'm an ideas guy. This means I can come up with an idea and then 10 versions of it as I start to add more creative energy to it.

That said, I'm not somebody who needs to be right. Therefore, if I sense, or am told, that an idea is wrong, I'm totally open to reviewing, altering or ditching it.

My mind isn't the only thing that changes in our business. Changing team members and service providers is inevitable. Partly because my business continues to evolve, it requires people with new and different skill sets. This may be because somebody on the team has a change in their personal life that influences their overall level of commitment. As soon as this happens, it's time to discuss a change. Sometimes it can be sudden and other times it can be premeditated. Either way, a good rule of thumb is that if a relationship is broken and no longer serves the team, then it may be time to end it.

I prefer no gaps when it comes to transitions between relationships, whether staff, service providers or my own career. I want to know who my new employee or service provider is in advance of saying goodbye to whomever I have currently.

I owe it to my team to not be too sudden or drastic in my actions whenever possible. Drastic is reactive, whereas proactive change allows for behind-the-scenes preparations, including time to discuss and review options, to ensure any transitions are as seamless and comfortable as possible.

KEEPING A GOOD TEAM

For me, creating a good team is about smart selection and having the right DNA or personality in each team member to provide support as needed. Keeping good people around is simple. Here's what works for me.

Treat people well

At conferences and company functions, our team is often questioned (individually, over in a corner with drinks in hand) about our secret sauce.

Everybody wants to know how we stay together, how I provide compensation, how we share leads, how we share responsibility, how they handle working with me.

One of my assistants, a dear friend, once responded to the "How do you guys do it" question with a brilliant one-liner. I think the guy who asked her was actually trying to steal her as an assistant. She responded by telling him, "The whole secret to finding great people to work for you is be great to work for."*

Pay people well

Good things happen when people can pay their bills. The more we know about each other and our hobbies and interests, the more we can support each other to ensure we are winning in as many areas as possible. I like to bonus frequently and sporadically, and at times have let people set their own salaries. I can assure you the value I get from a happy staff far exceeds the money I spend on keeping them happy.

'Date' the team

Another key to our team staying together is that I often refer to each and every team member as somebody that I am dating. In fact, we're all "dating" each other. This is different than marriage in that I think marriage has an elevated level of commitment, while in dating anybody can leave at any point without a whole lot at stake.

We'll meet often and go for coffee or lunch to check in. We ask each other what's working and what's missing from our relationship. Typically I want to know if there's anything I have committed to or promised that hasn't been followed through

---

* Thank you Julie for that very kind compliment.

on. This can range from compensation to personal family matters that need to be discussed. We are here to support each other to be the best versions of ourselves. That's how we can support the rest of the team. The same relationship-building we apply to clients apply to our staff too.

As the team leader, it's really about being intuitive and tuned in to my team members. One-word check-ins, which we do at every meeting, can reveal a tremendous amount. If you ask a team member to sum up their current state in a single word, imagine how much you can learn if they say "exhausted" instead of "excited."

I'm never afraid to care about the individual and what they have going on outside of our business. I don't think my business and personal life are in any way mutually exclusive. It's my job to care and support my team on all levels.

Conclusion

THAT'S IT, BUT IT'S FAR FROM ALL

I feel like one of the most fortunate guys on Earth. I hope I've made it clear that I didn't get where I am due to luck. There's no such thing as luck, but even if there were, it would be out of our control. What we can control is hard work, preparation and seeking out opportunities.

The other thing in my control is how thankful I am for the life I have. I'm thankful I'm alive, thankful I live in the place I do, and thankful I was born when and where I was born.

I'm thankful that I've had people show me how to turn obstacles into opportunities.

I'm thankful that I learned how to hustle rather than wait for someone else to do it for me.

Maybe, above all else, I'm thankful I have the mom and family I do.

Every day is really a day to start again. If you're reading this page because you've read everything that came before it, you may find that tomorrow is a day you'll get to start again. To start again with whatever you've learned in this book, but also everything you've experienced, felt and succeeded at in the days before.

I'm determined as hell to turn tomorrow into something better than yesterday in each area of life that really matters to me. Along the way, I plan to have fun, be faithful, build a great team and help as many people as I can along the way.

I wish you the best of health because the rest is relatively in your control. I wish you all of the success you can handle, plus just a little bit more.

Positively,

Dennis Plintz

ACKNOWLEDGEMENTS

I can't say thank-you enough to the people who have helped me in the past and continue to do so for me in midlife, but I am committed to give it my very best shot before my days are up.

First off, thank you Mom for instilling in me the ability to forget the sour and focus on the sweet. We've tasted sour and we've tasted it at times by the mouthful. Although I'll never forget the taste, I will always look to appreciate every bit of sweetness that this life offers. You've taught me that.

Thank you to my brother. Through thick and thin you have my back. I know this and I'm thankful for it. Here's to the future.

My wife. I love you for so many reasons. Above all else you are my support at every level and you have taught me the power of believing in someone by giving support. Despite the size of my ideas or the complexity, you are the first to say, "Yes you can," and "Yes you should try." Somebody once said to us that I am the hood ornament and you are the engine. That about sums it up perfectly.

Caleb. Our first-born. You're my best teacher yet.

My extended family. Fortunately, but unfortunately, you are too numerous to mention by name. You've loved me through all of it and continue to shower me with support, encouragement and opportunities that keep me believing that better is always possible. I love you.

My first business forum group. Colin (Yoda), Cary and Don. Here"s to the cormorants that we are. And my extended forum. Leith, Lee, Frank, Norman, Chip and Jeff. The lessons and belief that each of you have instilled in me have made an immeasurable difference. Thank you for being leaders through good times and bad.

My team.

Danielle Reneau. You are so much more than somebody that gets shit done for our team. (Although that's true and you do it better than anybody I've ever worked with.) You care about me, my family and the business at a level that exceeds expectations. Anyone connected to you is very fortunate.

And directly connected to you, Danielle, is Zoey Duncan. That kismet event called Rollercon that changed my life in so many ways. Most of those ways were not to be mentioned in this book, but the one that has is the introduction to you, Zoey. This book and the next level of achievement that I believe is possible would not have been possible without you. Thank you.

Luke Nichols. Your loyalty and care for each and every aspect of what we do and who we are as people is massive. Keep being you and your success is unlimited.

A few people and team members past and present that helped me get started in this business and are the reason I can't imagine looking back: George Bamber, Brett Mote, Peter Stewart, Janet Mericle, Sylvia Falk, Stirling Davidson, Shirley Schwartz, Vicki Humphries, Steve and Kyle Bottoms, Anh and Tusha Hong, Julie and Steve Dierkens, Justin Mah, Lyndon and Rebecca St. John, Nigel Goodwin, Ross McCredie, Kyle Dunn, Mary-Anne Mears, Blake Burns, Shaun Connell and Chris Wiersma.

From fashion tips to structuring high-level financial deals and even aspects of my faith, each of you is way more than somebody I work with. You are friends and that makes this the most special business I could imagine working in.

Bring on the next chapter.

ADDITIONAL RESOURCES

Hungry for more information? Here are some of my favourite inspiring and knowledge-packed reads.

Over the Top by Zig Ziglar (Thomas Nelson)

Awaken the Giant Within: How to Take Immediate Control of Your Mental, Emotional, Physical and Financial by Tony Robbins (Free Press)

The Icarus Deception: How High Will You Fly? by Seth Godin (Portfolio)

Love Wins: A Book About Heaven, Hell, and the Fate of Every Person Who Ever Lived by Rob Bell (HarperOne)

The Little Big Things: 163 Ways to Pursue Excellence by Tom Peters (HarperBusiness)

The 10X Rule: The Only Difference Between Success and Failure by Grant Cardone (Wiley)

Crush It!: Why Now if the Time to Cash in on Your Passion by Gary Vaynerchuk (HarperStudio)

How to Win: Achieving Your Goals in Extreme Conditions by Cary Mullen (Mullennium Enterprises Inc.)

The Millionaire Real Estate Agent by Gary Keller, Dave Jenks, and Jay Papasan (McGraw-Hill Education)

Losing My Virginity by Richard Branson (Virgin Books)

Think and Grow Rich by Napoleon Hill (Ballantine Books)

Head to DennisPlintz.com/hustle for the latest details and presale information on forthcoming titles by Dennis including a guide for homebuyers and sellers that tackles all those crucial questions you absolutely need to ask your real estate agent that most people don't even think about, and a handbook specifically written for real estate agents who are ready to accelerate their careers and perfect their **HUSTLE.**